Literary Failure
and My Contribution to It

Literary Failure
and My Contribution to It

by

Stephen Wade

ODD VOLUMES

of the
Fortnightly Review
LES BROUZILS
2017

© 2017 Stephen Wade. All rights reserved.

Odd Volumes of
The Fortnightly Review

Editorial:
Château du Ligny
2 rue Georges Clemenceau 85260
Les Brouzils, France

info@fortnightlyreview.co.uk

ISBN-10: 0-9991365-1-8

ISBN-13: 978-0-9991365-1-5

PREFACE

This collection of excursions into social and cultural history, with some literary paranoia along the way, has its origins in my early years as a writer, when I was assured by my alter ego, a cross between Dostoievski and an Elizabethan sonneteer, that I was The Next Big Thing in poetry and the world was waiting for me. I was very wrong of course. Even the small magazines were not waiting for me. Nevertheless, I persevered and had some very small success writing for some of the smallest of small literary journals such as *Littack* and *Orbis*.

This was back in the days when we scribblers wrote on typewriters and used little strips of Tippex for the correction of typos, and there was no internet where one might check on everything in the vast world of knowledge, from Greek mythology to the anatomy of stag beetles. Then, c. 1970 when I first wrote reviews and little essays, one had to have reference books, and I have always loved and collected these, in revolt against the Google brain.

Persistence brings the mass of rejections but of course it also brings tiny scraps of encouragement, and it was when I reflected on this early phase of writing that I recalled two editors who were a wonderful help to me. These were Gregory Lomax, literary editor of *The Catholic Herald*, and Richard Mayne, who was in charge of film reviews and poetry at *Encounter*. These gentlemen actually accepted some of my work and urged me to send more contributions. It was the uneasy balance between failure and success that led me to write this book.

It could not have seen the light of day, however, without the encouragement of another literary gentleman, Denis Boyles, at the *Fortnightly*. It has been a delight to see the work develop in instalments- something I have never had before in my long writing career. Of course, when I tentatively submitted this to Denis, I expected rejection. That is the secret of a healthy and long life as a hack: expect nothing and be surprised.

The book does indeed celebrate the hack, the jobbing writer and the aspiring *litterateur*; along the way it throws up the occasional desperate lament on the vagaries of the writing life; but on the whole, we scribblers would do nothing else. We have a compulsion to write, and that may have nothing at all to do with the vanity of the author, who dreams of his name in lights as well as on the spine of a book.

We live in a very different publishing and writing world to that which existed when I set sail for the Isles of Words half a century ago; today, editors and agents are mercilessly assailed every day by people dreaming of celebrity success. The publishers and agents are drowning in a sea of synopses and sample chapters. Writers are being educated in such skills as the art of the query letter or the successful pitch. Somewhere beneath all the hype and the stress there is the pleasure of writing: the sharing in a story or a line of thought of writer and imagined reader, or indeed the pleasure of the dialogue with oneself which is also in the nature of putting the right words in the right order, building paragraphs and then crafting finished pieces.

With these thoughts in mind, I invite the reader to share my venture into the harsh world of literary rejection, a place whose denizens surely share one of Dante's purgatorial circles. I have lived there, and over the years I have made the acceptance of failure more of a hobby than a dark place of the soul.

I must end this preface with some words of assurance to those who may be experiencing their first rebuffs at the hands of editors. The words are simple: learn to see rejection as an invitation to astonish and surprise where you have previously only bored.

TABLE OF CONTENTS

1. The Rejected Authors' Chat-Lines 1

2. Being Philosophical About It 13

3. Gigs Gone Wrong: Rejection 'Live' 31

4. Before Rejection Slips 47

5. Self-Publishers and Self-Promoters 67

6. The Play's the Thing 93

7. Case Studies in Rejection and Success 107

8. Being Professional 131

9. Even the Famous and Successful are Rejected 141

10. Bad Reviews 153

1

THE REJECTED AUTHORS' CHAT-LINES

The twenty-first century is, from one perspective, a place where the media constantly generate the notion of support for the individual. Big Brother and his mechanisms of information ensure that any conceivable problem will be remedied by some kind of support system. You have one leg shorter than the other? No problem: The Shorter Leg Society, funded by bungee-jumps and back-waxing afternoons in the coffee shop, will offer support. You have a tendency to nod and agree too much when interviewed? No problem: the Affirmative Repetition Syndrome Network will provide sessions in which you are taught to stop nodding and to say 'yes' only when really necessary.

Authors too, have need of support. This is because they know rejection like they know a difficult lover; they want success and the Beloved rebuffs and dismisses them. All they ask for is a smile and a nod, and the lover to say, 'I love your work and I'll publish it immediately.' The smile does not come. The lonely author has to tread doggedly once again to that little box with the PC in it, and the new blank page, the page waiting for the next failure. But help is at hand.

The massive machinery of modern comfort and reassurance is there and is growing. Every conceivable modern malaise is dealt with in the plots of TV soaps, except arguably, the lot of the rejected author, but that will come. Any day now, Cain Dingle from *Emmerdale* will try his hand at love poems, have them rejected and then stand on the edge of a cliff wondering whether he can go on.

This is quite a new situation. History shows us that for centuries, authors were pathetic, marginal creatures just one level up from beggars and riff-raff. When they did become reasonably respectable, their professional nomenclature was still nowhere near being acceptable for any alternative occupation for the third son of the wealthy man, following the usual options of the law and the church. Septimus, the seventh son, might perhaps have considered the option, but would not have told papa of the plan.

If Septimus or Octavius failed as an author, Daddy would probably not pay up and publish the 30,000 line epic poem just to launch his progeny on a literary career. No, he would thrash him and find him a junior position in the office of Daniel Drudge, envelope-addresser of Armpit Lane.

Women had it even worse of course. Aphra Behn, one of the very first female authors, (1640-1689) had experience that most writers would give their best advance for, being a spy for Charles II in the Netherlands. But the problem was that she set out as a dramatist, having her first success with *The Forced Marriage* in 1670: that meant that, as she was working with the theatres, she was no better than a whore. Her path to authorship was not easy; some attacked her as a plagiarist and some were just plain envious of her success. The point is that she had to write, as we all do, alone, accessing her imagination and working hard to please the readers or the audience in the playhouse. If she needed listeners, or even a sorority, it was not there.

Before her time, back under the Tudors, being a writer was as dangerous as attending the wrong church service or saying the wrong thing about the king and his women, or the queen and her lack of progeny. A scribbler could find himself facing the axe or being pressed to death under a board if he wrote the wrong things. Who was there to help poor old Will Shakespeare when he was rejected? He must have been told to go away and improve. It seems likely that after submitting his first ink-stained manuscript, some theatre manager said '*Go and learn from Kit Marlowe mate... he's got the golden touch.*' Yes, he had, but look at what happened to him- murdered in a pub in Deptford.

One day -and that day is not so far away- there will be adverts in the tabloids offering help and advice to the rejected author. Cain and his ilk will be able to pick up the mobile and talk to an expert. The conversations will go something like this:

Putting You Write with Trudie Tease

    Writer: Hello, is that Trudie?
    Trudie: Yes sweetie... you saw my ad in the paper?
    Writer: Yes... *Cry on My Shoulder, Unwanted Poets*?
    Trudie: That's right. Now, tell me about it dear.

REJECTED

Writer: Well, it's the *twentieth* one.. I've been turned down twenty times. I'm crap.

Trudie: Oh no, my love, no you're not. What it is, my sweetie, it's that you're before your time, like Jimmy Joyce.

Writer: You helped James Joyce?

Trudie: Oh yes, he wept buckets, down the phone. I had to talk him out of suicide, my love.
Now, what didn't they like? Dodgy rhyming couplets?

Writer: Nothing specific …they hated it all – every one of my eighty-eight sonnets.

Trudie: Is the book called *Two Fat Ladies*?

Writer: Pardon?

Trudie: Never mind… just a joke.

Writer: (angry) What? You mean I'm here with a bottle of paracetamol and a crushed ego and you're cracking jokes? I'll call someone else… I'll ring that Sadie on
The Hot in the Attic line, they understand there.

Trudie: Ha! I know that Sadie… she's insincere.
Now look, I'm sorry I joked.
Please don't lose your self-belief. You're a great poet…

Writer: Are you sure?

Trudie: Course. If you want to go any further with me dearie, then go to
Our website and sign up to our little group- it's called *Many a Slip*.

Writer: (weeping) thanks Trudie… I'll talk to you again.

Trudie:	Yes, now here's a kiss for you, all the way from me, here at the end of the Line.
Writer:	End of the line? Does that apply to me? Trudie? You still there?

Chatter on Chatterton, Sweetie - Don't Top Yourself

Writer:	Is that Penny Pert?
Penny:	Of course my lovely, now put down the tablets, you don't need them.
Writer:	How did you know?
Penny:	See the name of my chat-line? That says it all.
Writer:	Sorry….. oh, I didn't notice you were sort of …like Samaritans.
Penny:	Yes, we're named after the tragic young poet… the marvellous boy!
Writer:	Well, I'm upset, but not that upset.
Penny:	They all say that. Now, what did the nasty publisher say?
Writer:	Said I was no good.
Penny:	What *exactly* did he say?
Writer:	That I was shit… not in so many words.
Penny:	Go on, read it out… you know you want to.
Writer:	Okay, I've got the letter here… ' Dear Mr. Proddy, after careful consideration We have decided that although your novel has a smack of realism, the plot is not convincing and the characters leave a lot to be desired. Your mss. lacks emotional velocity and pace. We suggest you take a

	course in creative writing or consult *The Writers and Artists Yearbook…*
Penny:	Now, sweetest one, that's not really a total rejection is it?
Writer:	'Tis…. Says I'm shit. I sweat blood over that bloody pile of trash… I didn't sleep for weeks….what's the point of it all?
Penny:	Now… what's your name by the way?
Writer:	Wolfram… Wolfram Weg.
Penny:	(*trying to stifle a laugh*) Oh I see…
Writer:	(*Slamming phone down*) Right… enough.

That's the end…

Relieve Yourself

Writer:	Hello… say it again will you? Like you did last time..
Prof.:	Oh it's you Harold
Writer:	Professor Paulina, say the line, for God's sake!
Prof:	Okay but this is the last time. You have to learn to be independent.
Writer:	SAY IT!
Prof:	Give me an iambic pentameter, you deviant poet
Writer:	Oh that's better. I can write now. I feel radical.
Prof:	Yes but it's not the remedy Harold. You need other people. Writers need to mix, to be well… human.

Writer:	Not all of us Prof. I only need you. You fulfil all my yearnings, Professor… I dream about you, I write sonnets about you… I need your voice Like… like….like…
Prof:	On shit… the block again. A simile, give me a simile….
Writer:	Like a ….like a…. like a
Prof:	Give me a simile, you deviant poet.
Writer:	Like I need fish and chips.
Prof:	I'm putting the phone down Harold. Don't ring again.

Yet, in spite of this rather fanciful opening, I have to switch to realism mode and make it clear that a survey of literary rejection opens up for scrutiny the very heart of the profession. Why? Because, as any writer will admit after a few drinks, they have heaps of unwanted, unfinished, unloved, unsupported, unseen manuscripts somewhere in their office. It is the most constipated profession- the writer holds on to every scrap of writing, usually kept on one of a thousand flowery note-pads bought in Waterstones with a resolution to use it for 'the masterpiece.'

Not only do we have rejection: we have failure in degrees. There is ordinary, everyday failure and then there is spectacular failure. The latter is art of the very highest order. To fail with style, panache and chutzpah is to achieve something very special.

A spectacular failure leaves an aftermath, a sense of shock or horror. The real specialists in this are those writers who insist on attempting the impossible, the Eddie the Eagles of literature.

Examples would be projects such as a 800-page history of Middle Topham in rhyming couplets; a tragedy in five acts, with copious stage directions, on Petronius Agrippa's youngest son, and perhaps an erotic novel titled *Hot Desire*, about a sex mechanic called Harry Hot on the loose in Sunderland.

In the first centuries of book production, authors made a notable effort to avoid failure by having long explanatory sub-titles, such as:

Godde's Grete Gobbets of Griefe

Being an account of sodaine spasms, horrid
hede-cracking agues
And famous classical deths all ascribed to that most
parlous sinne,
Fornication, as practised by subtile and cankered
strumpets in
The citie of Londonne, to the eternal shame of
gode-thinking folk.

*Written by Pastor **Wrestling Whitebones**,*
Sometime preacher to the Kynge of Spayne

A clear example of spectacular failure is the work of John Armstrong (1709-1779) who insisted on producing a poem entitled *The Art of Preserving Health*, which delights in describing the human gut, but some of his line, although encased in infinite tedium, hit hom to today's world, as in these words from 'Advice to the Stout':

The irresoluble oil,

*So gentle late and blandishing, in floods
Of rancid bile o'erflows: what tumults hence,
What horrors rise, were nauseous to relate.
Choose leaner viands, ye whose jovial make
Too fast the gummy nutriment imbibes...'*

It take class to create such a revoltingly wrong piece of work. Most writers have some vague notion of what subjects are likely to cause rejection and down-hearted dejection. But a few great souls have dared to go where none have gone before in this. Fortunately, many of the best worst writers have only ever seen their work on gravestones. Such a one was Cornelius Whur, who is responsible for this:

'He resteth where the nettles spring,
Not having aid from thee'

Equally, the work of that writer, anonymous, cries out for evaluation as failure, as in:

*Earth from afar had heard Thy fame,
And worms have learnt to lisp Thy name.'*

In fact, the one notable omission from my thematic history is Anonymous. He/she has perpetrated a whole canon of failures which cannot be included in my history. But one notable exception has to be made. These lines are the very definition of spectacular failure:

' O never, never she'll forget
The happy, happy day
When in the church, before God's priest,
She gave herself away.'

We poor souls languishing in the dungeons of rejection have to cling on to that hope that one day soon, the help-lines will open for us. Then Anonymous will have his/her day.

History also shows that failure steals up on the writer, unsuspected. The usual scenario is that the hapless hack has a wonderful idea, something that will be the magnum opus. The time seems right, the writing appears to be excellent, your friends say your work is marvellous, and there is no thought of the work being rejected. Then it comes when least expected, a slim letter hidden in a tranche of mail on the mat, nestling between a flyer for the new pizza take-away and a tax demand.

As time pressed on and publishing became established as a money-making notion, writers became a nuisance. Basically, there were too many of them. Most failed scribblers could be picked out in society by their flat noses, caused by the door slamming them against the wall as they loitered outside a patron's door. With literary failure came its trappings and side-effects: most affected areas of the body were the bottom (writers' bottom' entered the medical vocabulary in the nineteenth century); the pen-pusher's palsy (affecting the cheek, which twitches after too much false smiling at agents) and most deadly of all, depression of course, brought on by rejection, and known as the 'sighing sickness.' This was caused by too much automatic sighing through boredom and misery.

But, as the following chapters will show, the help-lines were always going to come. Before they existed there was simply the shrink:

Scene: the sofa in Dr Mendham's therapy centre

Writer: So I wake up and the letter gradually dis solves, but it comes back during Day... I can't concentrate for the damned thing...

Shrink: Is there a heading? I mean, which company is it from?

Writer: Some long name..... They write that 'though my work shows promise, there are too many novels dealing with bestiality around at the moment...

Shrink: Bestiality? Could you explain please, Harold?

Writer: Well, my book... it's about two buffalo... back in the time of Custer' Last Stand.

Shrink: I'm not clear what...

Writer: Well that's the point... these are the last two buffalo left on the plains... in the whole world. Hence the title.

Shrink: Which is?

Writer: Custer's Last Stand. Custer is the male buffalo you see.....

Shrick: What? That's disgusting. You write about the sexual congress of Buffalo... why?

Writer: Somebody has to Doc. Don't they?

2

BEING PHILOSOPHICAL ABOUT IT

A Personal Confession

I begin with a statement of my own failure. I am in the fairly unusual position of having had experience of setbacks and duds in a rich variety of genres and forms. The reason for this is that I have had four phases in my writing career, and there has been a distinct mix of flops and false starts in each one:

Phase One: Poet

Failure here was in the extreme form, which is to say, a rejection slip tended to trigger a sequence of deep sulks, followed by kicks on inanimate objects and imbibing too much cherry brandy (I had no money so I accessed my mother's drinks cabinet). At this stage, I was not aware of Alexander Pope's guidance regarding bad poetry. He explained that getting poetry out of the system was a handy prelude to trying proper writing: ' It may be affirmed with great truth, that there is hardly any human creature past childhood, but at one time or another has had some Poetical Evacuation, and no question was much the better for it in his health…'

Phase two: Hack essayist

Having attracted interest from Faber and Faber but then been rejected by them, I switched to pontificating on poetry and writers generally. At this stage I was an insufferable bore, a poetaster who behaved like a Professor. Rejections were more wordy, but still lethal. Result: rants and red faced- loathing of all periodicals who refused my work.

Phase three: True Crime Writer

Fate and circumstances led me into the role of crime enthusiast. That is, I developed and unhealthy interest in bloody murder from years long gone. I actually did very well in this, but found that, when I acquired an agent, all the ideas for stories I was burning to tell met with rebuffs from large publishers. Reason: there were too many other writers doing the same thing.

Phase Four: Magazine Contributor

At some point I wandered into writing for history and regional magazines. At first I seemed to attract a few acceptances in between the rejections, but then all the doors closed against me.

Today, though I exist as a general non-fiction writer, my most detailed specialist subject, should I ever be called to appear on

University Challenge, is literary failure. Hence this book. Rejection is many things, if we search for images to explain it: like being hit by an iced-water spout; being slapped in the face by a wet haddock; being pole-axed by a thump to the midriff; being told to get off the pitch and have an early bath.

At the very heart of the experience, the really dark, destructive experience is that one feels excluded from a nice, cosy, chummy club. One sees them being interviewed for the Hay Festival, these professional writers, sitting on sofas looking cultured and confident; they appear on TV when it's Valentine's Day or World Book Day, and one has this feeling that they all go away, back to a life of chatting about their chapter four in a London coffee-shop. They put in an hour or so in the office and then start tweeting and blogging and they have a following of thousands, groupies who want to collect their spittle and their sweat. Sometimes they have to sit in a bookshop and sign their name on a book that they have written, and people queue to gaze on them and ask for the book to be signed to 'Cathy' rather than 'Catherine' so that they can say they are bessie mates with the author.

But the rejected author is not good enough for this media world. The rejection letter shuts them out in the cold, condemning them to another year's hard labour at the screen, sitting at the kitchen table on a Sunday night, before they have to be up and away to do their 9-5 job the next morning.

The rejected author is not an author. When asked by friends how their book is coming on, they have to try to smile and say that the publisher didn't want it. Excuses have to be found, such as, 'It wasn't right for their lists' or ''The theme is unfashionable now' and one has to say this because otherwise one would lose face and then not be described as 'a writer' any more when introduced. In my younger days, I was sometimes referred to, at parties, as 'Steve, who's a teacher but he's a poet as well...' The following conversation would always be about the poetry, not the teaching.

My confession is that, earlier in my writing career, I burned with envy at those writers glorying in their fame, being loved and treasured by their readers, media darling, members of the glitterati, speakers and storytellers- while my stories lay untold, in the dark oblivion of my desk drawer.

Today things are very different. I have no envy, no rankling hatred and no brooding implosion of depression brought on by rejection. Rejections today flip over me like bats at dusk. I only weep when alone. Otherwise, the brave face is well practised and appears very easily and smoothly.

We seasoned scribblers gradually learn that the path to being a real writer is littered with rejection slips. It's rather like a boxer, having to learn the trade by sparring. The only difference is that we rarely have a chance of landing an uppercut on the jaw of the bastard who rejected the novel. I mean that in a *nice* way, just as they mean their rejections in a nice way too.

One tiny benefit remains to explain: it can be useful. That is, being rejected provides a talking point. There's always lots of support, plenty of comforting things said,... women feel sympathy for you. Though, as a chat-up line it has its limits:

'Hi... I'm Steve.'
'What do you do?'
'I'm a writer.'
'Oh really? What have you written?'

'Er... nothing. I've been rejected.'

If no sympathetic noises follow, one might say, 'But I've been rejected by Faber and Faber!' Not many can say that, you add.

Everyone you meet in the world of writing and publishing seems to have a story about J K Rowling's first Harry Potter book being rejected. The internet has a massive amount of material relating to literary rejection, and when the *Writers' Relief* site set about listing some classic rejection statements they included one for Rudyard Kipling: 'I'm sorry, Mr Kipling, but you just don't know how to use the English language' and a note sent to Emily Dickinson, one of America's greatest poets: ' Your poems are quite as remarkable for defects as for beauties and are generally devoid of true poetical qualities.'

The listings, at www.writersrelief.com/blog/2011/ provoked a huge response of over twenty pages of comment for writers, many seemingly convinced that it was all about taste anyway, and that a lot of writing in print was very poor. It's all a matter of opinion, of course, but when the lone writer receives the rebuff then it really hurts. A rejection is more than a blow to self-esteem and one's talents: it slaps down your sense of self.

Coping with rejection is now almost a science. It even provokes writers to coin their own technical terms, as in Mindy Klasky's notion of 'rejectomancy' which is, roughly, the skills involved in divining exactly what is meant by the wording of a rejection letter. Klasky analyses such phrases as 'Didn't grab me', 'Didn't hold me' and 'Didn't work for me.' She quite rightly surmises that there are clues in the coded expression of such formulaic phrases.

Changing Rejection Scenarios

Through all the years in which writers have submitted manuscripts for consideration, there has been the agony of waiting for a response, followed by the terror of the rejection, leading to the sheer evil hatred set against those who appear to have success on a plate. The failed writer has a tranche of excuses: *she has influential friends; she sucks up to everyone; she's got there by the casting-couch; she looks great and I need air-brushing...* and on and on. We writers refuse to accept that we might not be up to scratch, but then, some of the classic greats were not either.

I like to think that a note, accompanied by a bulky package of manuscript, dropped into a certain letter-box:

> *Dear Mr Joyce,*
> *We thank you for your manuscript of your work, Finnegan's Wake. Unfortunately, this does not fit easily with our current lists. It is hard to envisage how we could possibly brand your writer's identity based on this, although your title does hint possibly at a mariner's yarn and could be placed alongside the novels of Captain Marryat and Joseph Conrad. Our suggestion is, most importantly, that you pay attention to checking your grammar and punctuation before submitting this elsewhere..*

This, as all scribblers will know, is a letter of rejection. It is part of the learning process of those who dedicate their lives to the written word. The phrases at the opening of such brief notes are familiar to all those who feel the anguish of rejection. Here are a few opening gambits from those in power:

> *We regret that we cannot....*
> *Unfortunately, this is not for us...*
> *Your work has merit but....*
> *The coffee stain on p.5 was off-putting...*
> *We suggest that you try a publisher interested in German Shepherds...*
> *The market for this genre is difficult at the moment...*
> *We all enjoyed reading this but....*
> *Your manuscript entertained everyone in the office....*
> *Do not be discouraged but....*
> *Have you ever thought of voluntary work....*
> *Perhaps ten years from now attitudes may change...*
> *This was far too long....*
> *You have difficulty with pace....*
> *Our reader wilted at page 3003....*

Or, those gentle reviewers of writing may also crush and discourage the aspiring writer, as when William Wordsworth was told, on the publication of his magnum opus, *The Excursion*: 'This will never do....'

I have lived with rejection for almost forty years. I started my career writing sonnets about tulips and have progressed to producing biographies of obscure people from dusty old years gone by. But I sat down recently, taking stock of this long career of being rebuffed, and felt assured that my experience would help others, those new to the word trade perhaps. This book is my shadow autobiography, the story of the poet in me who never made it but stirred up some reactions in dark corners and forgotten by-ways of literature.

The scenario is familiar, that little narrative of rejection: phase one is the sense of impending doom when one realises that a bulky envelope has crashed onto the doormat; then phase two is the little voice inside saying, it may be an acceptance but with editing needed… Phase three follows: the placing of the envelope on the kitchen table and the mug of coffee placed near to hand. Finally, if there is another person near, you will ask them to open it, and they do, their face dropping and your own false smile sinking into a droopy expression of misery.

I have wept over manuscripts; I have trodden on them and wailed like a Cheyenne at a rain-dance; I have ripped them up with curses; I have held them with shaking grip and vowed never to write again; I have ranted like some head-case at anyone nearby about how I am misunderstood. I have even reminded myself, regularly, that even Will Shakespeare had rejections. I mean, in his later plays, they had to wheel in John Fletcher, winkling him out of the pub corner, to write the sex scenes after Will had been hit by depression sometime around 1602.

Of course, in the days before computers and the internet, there was the weighty package dropping onto the mat, but today there may simply be one line, such as 'Not for us.' Working as a freelance from home, writers become accustomed to curt rejections on e-mails, generally couched in diplomatic or bland terms. But even such brief responses are still horrendously damaging. Isaac Asimov called rejection slips 'lacerations of the soul' and he received them by post; today, we maybe want to agree with Neil Gaiman that 'When they tell you what they think is wrong and how to fix it, they are almost always wrong.'

But the deeply depressing problem is that they may be right, and that means seeing faults in your little darlings who have been sent forth into the cruel world of publishing.

Rejection - the fact is that it is too strong a word. We need others to apply. I suggest *possible postponement* or *partial decision* or *reluctant rebuttal*. What about *Suggested tactical readjustment?*

No, we must man up or woman up and apply some muscular Christianity here. They were the guys who could handle pressure and being rebuffed. Yes, those Victorian Muscular bible types could be told to buzz off by the Ashantis and the Zulu, told to take their speeches elsewhere, brand themselves with pokers on the bum, and what did they do? They wrote another speech and came back, ready to tell the benighted peoples of the Dark Continent that their writing and speechifying was top notch and boy they should read their latest tome entitled, *Selected Homilies for the Infidel* or *Little Bible Tales for the Heathen Masses*.

So, with all this in mind, on we go, into the by-ways of my social history as a shunned author, and through the history of literary rejection as well, but I have a message for all who have the obsession to write and publish- keep at it.

Of course, being rejected may be a blessing in disguise to writers; after all, being told by those in power that one's expertise may lie elsewhere is potentially good career advice. Not, one has to say, if the advice is to leave off writing entirely and the poor scribbler in question is a delicate soul. In many cases, the rebuff has led to new directions being adopted, and so the advice is sound and indeed, is a pointer to the writer's real strengths.

Yet, stories in the histories of writers' lives concerning the unpredictable consequences of failure, pack the story of literature from the very beginning. Urg, the caveman poet, must surely have scratched his pictorial account of the dinosaur hunt on the wall of his home, only to be greeted with a chorus of boos from the tribe and a general agreement that it wasn't like that at all, and it wasn't even Durg who killed the beast.

There are instances of rejection and its following dejection, being part of the future career which becomes hugely successful, as in the case of Isaac Asimov. In his case, rejection was never actually expressed; his first ever science fiction submission was merely lost to oblivion. No reply came his way. Was he dejected? Not at all. His career biography contains the startling fact that he produced, across many genres, over 600 titles.

Of course, silence is arguably the ultimate rejection: what could be worse for the struggling aspiring writer than a response to a submission which is nothing more than an enormous silence, a meaningful gap of time, with no response? Then the inevitable realisation by the writer that the work in question has been ignored, perhaps lost in a slush pile the size of Blackpool Tower, and that the destiny of the magnum opus is sheer oblivion. Worse, the feeling creates a shiver of fear: that in fact, the writing is so execrable that no verbal response is possible and that the editor has chosen to remain silent, and if pressed, to regret that 'the work never reached us here.'

Many writers will be familiar with the task of having to pen the 'reminder note' to the editor or publisher. It is a very difficult document to produce, requiring tact and control of the simmering anger beneath the query. This is the result of that conviction of extreme Angst, of internal turmoil and despair on the part of the poor writer, reduced to a sad little message something like this:

> *Dear Editor,*
> *Six months ago I sent you the mss. of my novel, Dangerous Denis, a novel of the Napoleonic Wars (it's the French version of Denis by the way). As yet, I have received no reply, and I am anxious to know whether or not you actually received the package containing my work. Could you please check that you have it and let me know that, should you have read it, you may have reached a decision as to its suitability for publication.*

Note the tone of quiet anxiety here, the wish not to offend, the desire to be cautious and inoffensive, the importance of not being noted as being the whining pest that you just know publishers dread. What the writer really wants to write is more like this:

> *Dear bastard power-mad editor,*
> *Where the------------ is my great novel of the Napoleonic wars? You've had It on your desk for six sodding months and it's only 200 pages so you must have read it. For Christ's sake speak to me! Don't tell me you've lost it or that it never reached you, because at the moment my ego is so fragile that I'm on the edge of unreason and life is so fine and dandy that I'm contemplating hurling myself under the next tube on the Northern Line.*

Reflections on Failure

Failure. That is a sledge-hammer word. In our ultra-sensitive world, where we try to protect every living species from the terrors of language, we avoid using it. A horse comes in last at the races: it's not a failure, it's a 'tryer' with an unlucky habit of struggling at the back. In the unenlightened past you could you could say that someone was a failure and not fret that you were risking prodding them to self harm or litigation, or even to depression and suicide.

But it is a word which cuts sudden and deep: *failure, failing, being failed...* This is a lethal member of that group of F words in the English language, emotionless thugs who loiter in the dark corridor of that neglected tower-block of our self-doubt. His friends are *flounder, flop, fudge* and *fumble*. F sounds match well with those nagging emotions inhabiting uncertainty, lack of faith in the self, tentative erosion of the ego.

It is even more deadly after its partner, silence, has caused a wearing, tormenting period of Angst – something familiar to all writers awaiting an editorial decision.

The conferences, workshops, magazines and web sites teem with advice to aspiring writers, offering tips on how to cope with being 'unaccepted' or 'unpublished.' *Failure* is excluded from the vocabulary of creative writing, and the long agony of silence in which publishers do not respond to scripts, is ignored. The poor writer sits there, enduring a condition without alleviation or remedy, waiting months for a response, in a great, dominating silence, a word-free space in his or her life in which adjectives describing the work in limbo enter the mind with increasing agony: words such as *predictable, flat, bland* or *hack-*

neyed. The persistent thought is, well, I've failed. It's a question of how they will explain that failure…

The writer's fragile ego is a vital factor of course: we are reportedly a delicate breed who yield to tears at the slightest hint of a negative reception of our wonderful words, the product of perhaps years of hard labour at the desk. But is this merely a myth? Surely rejection is so commonly experienced that the writer grows a carapace as thick as a brick? Not so. For many, even writing the opening sentence of the new novel brings that black shadow of failure over the scene. The completed work inevitably then prompts the writer to edit: out comes the red pencil and soon, that growing doubt increases to a belief that what has been produced is third-rate and will never be edited up to first-rate.

The ego is thin and brittle as filo pastry, and the consequences of rejection may be extreme. Offices have been wrecked and livers turned to stone by booze because of rejection- that callous and thoughtless refusal to accept the manuscript (seen through the eyes of the hapless writer that is). The denial of literary talent may be the negation of the artist's sense of self. But, after all, we're talking business, and in the writing game, the ringing tills win over the sighing writerly laments.

Hanging over the failed author, like the Sword of Damocles, is the sad tale of poet Thomas Chatterton, who wrote poetry claiming to be by an earlier poet, Thomas Rowley; he was loved and admired at first, but then, at the age of just seventeen, he took his own life by taking arsenic, living in terrible penury. It is of little importance that his work was written supposedly as being by an imagined writer. There is no plagiarism there, and he was still amazingly talented and creative. He had immediate success, followed by rapid and extreme failure, rejected by the cruel world he longed to join.

Deeper Thoughts on Missing the Mark

As Joseph Brodsky wrote: 'The sad truth is that words fail reality as well…' In other words, the creativity in writing is doomed to fail anyway – in the deepest sense that we fail to put on a page the perceptions and feelings we had that initially moved us to write. We all know that even the best writing – the classics of every form and genre- have failed, ultimately, to recreate on the page what existed in a pre-verbal form in the author's mind. All writers have had that crushing feeling: there has been a struggle to write exactly what emotional statement or insight has been felt, and still, after writing draft after draft, it is not right, not accurate. We have to accept that we work to get as close as we can to that pre-verbal perception. So in a philosophical sense, failure is inevitable.

But the gap between that kind of failure and the rejection slip is immense. T S Eliot understood this, as he shows in these lines from 'The Lovesong of J Alfred Prufrock:'

> *'If one. Settling a pillow by her head,*
> *Should say: 'That is not what I meant at all,*
> *That is not it, at all.'*

Yet, in spite of philosophy and its ruminations, there is still the persistent topic of 'bad writing.' The problem is that we all feel unsure how to define it. In the classic collection of failed poetry, *The Stuffed Owl* (1930), the editors, Wyndham Lewis and Charles Lee, admitted their uncertainty by writing that ' There is bad Bad Verse and good Bad Verse.' But at least they provided a list of those most likely to produce the bad Bad verse: The field of bad Bad Verse is vast and confusing in its tropical luxuriance. The illiterate, the semi-literate, the Babu, the nature-loving contributor to the county newspaper, the retired station-master, the spinster lady coyly attuned to Life and Spring, the hearty but ill-equipped patriot...' The editors are definitely biased and not a little unfair, working in dead stereotypes, but their point is that, as they put it later in their essay, that they 'warn the reader strongly against despising or patronising good Bad verse.'

All this means that, as far as rejection goes, there has always to be an element of taste. One critic's realism is another one's sentimentality. This is all very sensible and rational. But there is another element, a spiritual one. This introduces the subject of spiritual guidance. We need all the help we can get, including that from another, higher plane.

Our Patron Saint

Those in the lower depths of uncertainty, self-doubt and fear of being rebuffed need someone to pray to. St Jude is the patron saint of failures, but that general sense will not do. We need a saint who exceeded in achieving failure on a grand scale.

The rejected writer, perhaps more than any artist, needs words of comfort. They may not be wise words, but at least the poor scribe needs a listener. The writer is notorious for talismans. In my office I have a clutter of such objects, all supposedly bring beneficent feelings and assurance to me: a Hopi chain with Kokopelli the flute-player; the Sun God of Egypt' Ankh, the Roman owl Glaucus, pet of Minerva who looked after wisdom and creative sorts. I even have a cheap version of a Tudor poesy ring, and at least fifty cards pinned around the place with quotes, mantras and maxims from the wise. They have been useful but more is needed- something deeply spiritual.

We need a patron saint of rebuffed writers, to lead us through the following history, and a case could be made for Chatterton, but a more likely candidate comes to mind. My suggestion is Gilbert, and the man in question was first described by Stephen Pile in his book of 'Heroic Failures.' Pile notes that a certain Gilbert Young wrote a book called *World Government Crusade*. This was rejected 'by more publishers than any other single manuscript.'

Saint Gilbert be with us, we writers in search of fame, glory and most of all our name on the spine of a book. Saint Gilbert, perhaps assisted by Saint Charlotte Bronte, because she ignored the patronising claptrap of Southey and pressed on, writing in between the ironing, the cooking and looking after her dad when he was going blind.

What follows, as well as my own story, is an account of a forgotten path in modern social and intellectual history – the story of famous rejections in the ranks of our British authors, along with the unsung heroic life of someone (*moi*) who has tried to push words into every available crack in modern society- inspired by the unshakable belief that words are good for you and that sharing words with others is better than reading them when alone in some garret. Yes, he has tried and been rejected so often along the way – as all we scribblers have. Has the poor scribbler in these pages been wrong? Who knows? The activity of inflicting words in public has a very long history. The Anglo-Saxon Beowulf poet began his recitation with the word 'Hwaet!' This means, roughly translated, 'Now then, shut up and listen.'

I would never be so rude. Let me put it this way: Dear reader, I beg your indulgence in presenting you with lamentable stories of writers rebuffed, and also my own failures, my poor words, the shavings from the floor of that great wooden chest of language that is my literary life. Or, if you like, from that bin of rejection slips that has shadowed my literary struggles.

The following chapters will trace the growth of rejection, the plight of authors down the centuries, and will also contain some of my own experience as a man unwanted, shut outside and often cold-shouldered: a man, in short, who has the empathy to share setbacks and rebuffs with rejected authors everywhere.

3

GIGS GONE WRONG: REJECTION 'LIVE'

The Best-Laid Plans…

Arguably, the worst kind of rejection is having no-one interested at all. If this happens at a planned live performance, then the deflation is total. After all, this writing business is all about the ego. Orwell said that one of the main reasons for anyone writing was vanity. Yes, vanity: I have no problem with the word. All writers everywhere would agree: you want your name on the spine of that book, and you want to wander into the bookshop when it's in print and stand around, peeping across to see if anyone browsing the shelves might just pick it up. Oh yes, vanity is at the core of the job.

It was a very famous poet who set me thinking about the sheer strangeness involved in a 'reading' of literary effusions. The man in question had won several national awards for fiction and for poetry. He was a quiet Scotsman, wearing a mac like that worn by detectives in old movies, and he pulled on a dead cig all the time, in between the sad story. He had come to town to read in a rugby club, and my Head of Department had organised it all. All I had to do was look after him – keep him in whisky and optimism.

'Gigs can go wrong…' he said this laconically, like Philip Larkin without the aid of a bottle of whisky and an old church. 'Like the time I turned up… come down from Edinburgh for it… a poetry reading at this art centre. Didn't work out.' We were walking into the rugby club now, and I led him into a nice quiet room with all the cosy chairs set out ready, and a little stage made out of old crates that the Hon. Sec. had prepared earlier.

'No, Stevie boy… there was this bloke standing there with a bunch of keys like you'd need in Alcatraz. 'You the poet mate?' He asked. I nodded. 'Well, I've just locked up… not a soul in there pal. Cancelled.' He walked off into the night, and I stood there, my invoice in my pocket and my little ragged book of poems. Tragic, Stevie boy, tragic.'

Then, half an hour and three whiskies later, he was reading his lyric meditations on the crates. The first few readings were fine, but then through a thin partition we (the audience of four) could hear the crash and grind of pin ball machines and drunken prop-forrards singing bawdy ballads. The poor man went on, courageous and cheery, resolved to bring his imagination and with to bear on the benighted proles who could only manage a chorus of 'Oh Mrs McLusky she had us all in fits/ jumping off the mantelpiece and landing on her….'

I've never forgotten that, and every time I meet a writer who goes out on the circuit, I ask about gigs gone wrong. Since I started spreading words and collaring victims who might listen to my poems –in about 1975 I reckon – I've seen the lot, every shade of failure and every type of venue. I've stood up and read poems at Hull City Hall at Saturday lunch time when all the poor folk around just wanted to eat their pizzas in peace; I've read poems to an audience of three at a magnificent Tennyson celebration bash in Cleethorpes; I've read for an hour to one lady in a long, cold hall: a lady who fell asleep after my third sonnet. The absolute nadir of this was in Kirklees Central Library when I gave a talk on literature and three ladies walked into the room and started to wander around the shelves asking everyone where the Catherine Cooksons were? I carried on regardless, knowing that such absurdity was part of the baggage that comes with the trade.

So after reflecting on this experience, I decided to sit down and write a social history of my efforts to take words out into the middle of people's gatherings. I became what one man called a 'cultural shit-stirrer' early in my teaching career., and as time has gone on, my desire to read poems, put on plays and tell anecdotes to anyone who would sit and listen has intensified. It's all down to my certainty that literature will bring us together, although experience has taught me that it often makes a crowd disperse and run for the nearest bar.

I have been, over the last thirty years or so a Russian-Yorkshire poet, an aesthetic Wildean, a Nervalian *flaneur* inhabiting literary cafes, a stand-up embarrassment purveying Yorkshire dialect verse, and a writer walking the wings in prisons. All this activity springs from my love of the spoken word. I put it all down to hearing the great Irish poet W B Yeats, who ill-advisedly recorded his poem on some kind of early His Master's Voice disc, chanting 'I will arise and go now...' in a tone somewhere between a guy eager for the loo and a vicar giving a sermon on a cold Sunday in Upper Swagdale.

Before offering the chronicle of word-mongering that has been the backdrop to my life, I end my prologue with the warning to anyone who might be considering planning and delivering a serious poetry reading. It was around 1980, and the young man stood up in a crowded student union gathering to read his poem. The general theme was an exploration of the question as to whether or not life was worth living.

He began solemnly and declined into maudlin distorted philosophy, quoted everyone from Sitting Bull to Emmanuel Kant. The audience visibly sagged. Chins were close to the floor and some bolder types actually yawned and muttered to themselves. Finally, a character braver than average, or merely desperate offered advice to the poet: 'For God's sake, yes... top yourself then!'

Reading and performing

It was around 1960 when the first bright spark had the idea of having a poetry reading that entailed proper, entertaining, planned delivery of the written word. Roger McGough told me once that he worked out a 'set' – an order of reading, meticulously conceived, with an eye on the best opening and the best closure. There was none of that when I started out. It was a case of standing up, shuffling a wodge of paper around and saying, 'The first poem is.. well, it's about my dog. Well no, not exactly… more about my first meeting with the disabled guy in Clapham… Anyway here's the poem. It's called ' Opening Up.'

My first efforts deserved failure. I tended to spend hours deciding which poems to read, then marking the sheets at the top in red ink, with a number. So that was fine. Then, just before standing up, I fell foul of the nagging voice, familiar to all poets who stand up to read, of *Scheiss*, the Wagnerian sprite of doubt and criticism whose voice tells you that what you have on paper is garbage and that reading it aloud will be the death of you. Scheiss, a whispering and insidious git who raps your nerves with his Sword of Silence, reminds you that it's better not to read that… read something else. The result of all this? I shuffled, hummed, coughed, smiled nervously, and finally selected a poem, which I read as if I was a spotty kid standing up to read Shakespeare at a school event.

I had a poetic friend who used to talk for five minutes, explaining all the story behind the poem and then read a little *haiku* poem of three short lines. The general opinion of him was that he could leave out the poem and just tell the back story.

The greatest mistake, in those early days of serious readings, was to claim a philosophical expertise. We were all reading thinkers such as Marcuse and McLuhan, Sartre and Camus. So the average reading would begin with: ' Now behind this lyric is the uneasy dynamic of activism, and the undercurrent metaphor is struggling to express a dialogue hinged on the feminine in the author..' This invariably brought a shout along the lines of 'So it's a gay poem then?'

REJECTED

If we trawl through time and try to locate the beginnings of the literary reading, the discoveries regarding gigs gone wrong are fascinating. For some cultures, reading aloud has never been a problem: the Romans always read aloud, even when alone. Consequently, when it came to your Roman poet doing a little reading to win over his wealthy patron perhaps, so that cash could be found for a neat little vellum edition of the poet's odes, the performance was no problem. The only snag was that, with a glut of poets, there was heated competition. If we imagine our own poet from classical times, Marcus Pubic Lascivius, he may have held forth with something like this:

To Clamidia

Oh once vestal virgin,
Fallen woman with gorgeous hips,
I was once surgin'
With a pash for your lips.
One long summer
You tormented my Roman heart;
It sure was a bummer
When I saw you were a tart.

On once vestal virgin,
Fallen woman with a queue of men
Whose poxy parts need purging
Because they lay with you again
And again and again and again.

Oh once vestal virgin,
We could love once more, it's true;
Because my loins are surgin'
For one more night with you.

The debate following the reading may well have been a polite quiver of applause, but the back-biting and name-calling would have been rabid. After all, the mob of aspiring poets were fighting for the crumbs of patronage like sparrows after bread-crumbs. In the real world of Augustan poetry- the period under the Emperor Augustus, the poets around the great patron Maecenas, scholars have shown that there was a circle of poets gathered around the now famous names of Virgil and Ovid and that these lesser lights were either critics or targets of satire. But generally, the groups of poets lived by compliments more than criticisms, as in the case of Ovid, who called a poet called Rabirius 'mighty mouthed.'

Literary gigs really took off with Chaucer and his contemporaries; the author of *The Canterbury Tales,* who read his work aloud to the court of Richard II. At that time, the late fourteenth century, the traditional minstrels and their poems and songs were rather in decline, and along came the new breed like Chaucer, to entertain others (often at the table) with his contemporary stories. You can bet your last groat that even old Geoffrey had a few restless types in the audience. There would have been the odd heckler who asked when he was going to move on from Middle English and move into the modern age. There is no doubt that the last unfortunate minstrels had a tough time.

Being a minstrel was what Humphrey Bogart would have called a 'bum rap.' Here was a poet who was expected to deliver a set of around set songs in praise love, the Queen and the King, while avoiding the flying wish-bones and pigs' trotters from the wine-soaked hearties at the trough in front of him. All the poor guy had was a mandolin or a lute: no backing track, no dancing girls, no sweet play of lights on the stage to add some mystery.

No, merely the man and his strings – and his voice of course. Rejection for him was 'get off, we've heard that before!'

As their art became a little more sophisticated, they thought that anew name would help their fortune, so they began to be called 'jongleurs' and then 'troubadours' but the repertoire was frozen in time and still the animal bones and offal were hurled at them, until some of them wised up and added a heavy to the band, a man who had been in a few scraps and could look threateningly at the mad blades crazed with lust and hock in the pit, down where the hunting dogs were rutting and the mice eating scraps. No knickers were thrown at them, as such undergarments were not known at the time; the only items thrown with a sexy intent would have been perhaps table napkins stained with blood or loincloths with unspeakable provenance.

The Old Entertainers

Sir Walter Scott was intrigued by this decline in fortunes, and in his classic 1805 poem, *The Lay of the last Minstrel*, he pays tribute to these outmoded troubadours whose gigs started to go wrong when Geoff and his mates moved in. Scott's poem is sad from the opening lines:

> *'The way was long, the wind was cold,*
> *The minstrel was inform and old;*
> *His withered cheek, and tresses grey,*
> *Seemed to have known a better day....'*

A more modern tale, circulated in manuscript until discovered by an obscure Victorian scholar, recounts the plight of one of the last of the breed in a more contemporary idiom, when a gig went wrong. Here is the relevant extract from the story:

Ned, The Broken Jester

… times were desperate in 1390, for any old bard who had lost his audience. Ned found that his lute and elegies to past romantic attachments were no longer In demand, and in the notorious affair of the Bone-Clattering stag party, his sad demise was confirmed. Ned, being always bold in spite of his shivers of agony and tendency to wet his hose before a gig, bravely waited behind the curtain at Bone-Clattering Manor as Lord Batty Bone Clattering downed his tenth flagon of Rhenish and threw a bottle at the minstrel gallery, shouting, 'Bring on the the ragged old slack-arse poet!'

Ned, by this time alone in the world, with all kith and kin gone the way of all mortal beings (emigrated to Siberia to avoid his songs) gathered himself, tuned his lute and strode on, into view, above the revellers. At first, he had a dreg of hope, as he had chosen his most appealing poem to render the first line being the epic 'Of cutlery I sing…'

There was a nano-second of silence as the young louts absorbed the line, but what followed was the ultimate rejection of the jester, a man struggling beyond his time. ' Fire your crossbow at him Charlie' screamed the drunken youngest son of ten, 'I hate poets!' Ned, about to sing his bawdiest song instead, saw the bolt being loaded and the string pulled back, and ducked out of view in the nick of time, as the bolt thudded into the head of the stag beside him, making the antlers fall on the hapless jester's head.

Skalds, Bards and Storytellers

In the Dark Ages, the tribal bards obviously suffered mightily at the hands of the kings and heads of tribes. There are suggestions that reciting poems was a side-line of the poison-tester in the beer-hall, and that he also had to double as jester, which was always a tough cookie to crack. In fact, as in *King Lear,* the court comic's destiny could be wandering the wild heath telling corny jokes and flat one-liners. But the toughest task was the bard or skald's requirement to fulfil the job-description and provide a story in verse for the beer-swillers and roughnecks in the thane's band of thugs. One biography which has come down to us is that of Swartwulf, and his great poem –story on the Saxons begins with the memorable lines,

> 'From the distant sea our people came,
> Walking like lame seals, riding the water's back;
> The great thane Sidebottom did lead us,
> Making that gert big shire of York.....'

One great advantage the tribal bard had over the modern writer is that he was mostly performing for drunks; his audience was therefore rarely in command of any critical faculties, although objects could no doubt be hurled at a bard who was falling below any perceived standard of quality entertainment.

Dullness

The basic missing faculty which may be absent in failed writers is talent. Arguably, the main barrier to attaining that is a quality of dullness. The snag is that a poet may be dull and not know it. That's why critics exist. Though they may also be dull, so other critics are needed to tell them. But these critics may be dull so…That's why we have literary theory.

By the eighteenth century, as the great Alexander Pope reminded everyone, dullness in writers found a new low. In that great age of satire, there was undoubtedly a glut of mediocre talent amongst the scribblers. Most of them tried very hard to make their way in the world by writing in praise of anything they happened to come across, such as :

> *Oh tender trembling tippling tiny trotter*
> *I hate to eat you but I gotta*

Or perhaps they published poems to their friends, or at least, celebrities with whom they wanted to be friends, so that they could pretend they were successful:

> *Jack! Great bard of the west country, with a muse of fire,*
> *I salute thee and thy noble verse, tho' my own attempts are dire…*

The absolute masters of dullness found that they had a fame of sorts, as they were the target of much ridicule. Outstanding among these alleged inadequates were Colley Cibber and Thomas Shadwell. Cibber, well published, and quite a force in the theatre of his time (he lived from 1671-1757), was nevertheless thought to be hopelessly mediocre. He was deeply involved in the scraps and backbitings in the literary world of his time, and sadly, his verse has failed to inspire, and is not far behind the great McGonagall in flatness:

REJECTED

Tho' rough Seligenstadt
The harmony defeat,
Tho' Klein-Ostein the verse confound;
Yet, in the joyful strain,
Aschaffenburgh or Dettingen
Shall charm the ear they seem to wound

These noble lines are from his poem, 'Air.'

Shadwell, however, was hammered mercilessly for his failure to impress by the poet John Dryden in the seventeenth century. Dryden conceived of a Kingdom of Dullness, with MacFlecknoe as the King in need of an hair, so enter Thomas Shadwell: ' In prose and verse, was owned, without dispute/ Through all the realms of nonsense, absolute.' Dryden builds up to a template description of the poet failed through fatal dullness:

Shadwell alone my perfect image bears,
Mature in dullness from his tender years:
Shadwell alone, of all my sons, is he
Who stands confirmed in full stupidity.
The rest to some faint meaning make pretence,
But Shadwell never deviates into sense.'

This was the great age of the coffee house wits, when cliques and gangs gathered, keen to denigrate any perceived upstart. We might imagine a new aspiring poet on the scene, creeping into his corner seat, with full wig on his pate, lace-trimmed coat, and slim book of verse in hand, being observed by two war-horses of the literary world:

GIGS GONE WRONG: REJECTION 'LIVE'

Scene: Blind Todd's Coffee House, 1700

Scoff and tease sit in their usual seats by the fire, people-watching

Scoff: Look, my friend. 'tis that new bumpkin, thinks he's the bee's knees.

Tease: See how he pouts… beware, he may stand and read his latest ode!

Scoff: Heaven forfend! I heard he has a stutter.

Tease: (loudly) S…s… surely not my old f…f… friend Scoff?

Scoff: 'Tis said he has bedded Lady Spreadham and so he rises…

Tease: Hah! Rises you say? Methinks the upstart has no juice in him.

Scoff: Wait… he has seen up. Observe that wicked stare.. and he now turns up his nose.

Tease: He never will climb to fame… Lady Spread ham has slept with a hundred Coxcombs…

Scoff: Wait… who is this?
Enter John Dryden, who walks to the new poet and shakes his hand.

Tease: My eyes deceive me my old chum… Dryden warms to him!

Scoff: Surely he has not slept with Dryden. The man's straight as a carpenter's rule.

Tease: You think so? Think again. How do you think I got my pension from the King?

Scoff:	What"' stab me vitals! You have a pension from the King?
Tease:	Yes, two hundred smackers… did not I tell you?
Scoff:	No… damn you, Tease, I'm going to sit with Dryden's lot….

Classic Rejection

Robert Southey to Charlotte Bronte

Of all the Bronte sisters, Charlotte was the one who pushed to achieve publication. The three sisters, Charlotte, Emily and Anne, sat around the broad table in the Haworth parsonage while father Patrick amused himself with memories and guns across the hall. The sisters were eventually to find print, at their own cost, in the volume, Poems by Currer, Ellis and Acton Bell which arrived at the parsonage on 7 May, 1846, and caused a great thrill. Their need to have male identities as writers was unfortunate but essential in those benighted times for women poets.

Ten years before, with the dream of publication in her mind, Charlotte had written to Robert Southey, one-time romantic radical and now a comfy, establishment character who had accepted the laureateship. Charlotte wanted his opinion of her work, and the reply included these words: ' 'Literature cannot be the business of a woman's life and it ought not to be The more she is engaged in her proper duties, the less leisure will she have for it… Write poetry for its own sake, not in a spirit of emulation and not with a view to celebrity.'

She was shocked and rocked, so much that she wrote back: ' At the first perusal of your letter I felt only shame and regret that I had ever ventured to trouble you with my crude rhapsody… I trust I shall never more feel ambitious to see my name in print.' Oh yes? Well, Mr Southey, who reads your poem *Roderick the Last of the Goths* today, when they can open the pages of Jane Eyre and be sucked into a mesmerising story of a woman in search of her true self?

Today, the reader wants to give Southey a slap. That may seem extreme, but how dare he? The sad fact is that he was of the establishment, that magical, powerful elite who run the literary pages and awards, decide on the next big thing and control the review pages.

4

BEFORE REJECTION SLIPS

Writers and poets came long before publishers, agents and editors. The heart goes out to those first scribes who chipped words in rock or daubed on skins and were then lucky to have an audience of maybe one or two. It started as a family business. The wife would say, forcing the children to stare at a little haiku on the dinosaur skin mat, 'Look what your father's written, children. It's about that smelly creature he stuck with his spear the other day… isn't it lovely?' Or, the husband would say, to the good wife who had stitched a line of Zen poetry in his new vest, 'Look children, your mother's written a poem… about a flower. Isn't it great?' Knowing that their dinner depended on a favourable criticism, the little mites would smile and hug the parents, walking off to mutter, 'Er..gross!' behind the community peeing-ditch.

Literary failure comes in many forms. Editors and publishers, we suspect, like to think of innovative ways to say that we scribes are rubbish and that we ought to go back to the day-job sweeping up litter or peeling kebabs. But the 'rejection slip' or 'rejection e-mail' is the offending communication. Stealing up unobserved sometimes, and at other times slamming you like a clout from Arnie when he's come back again. At its most deadly, it arrives couched in deceptively cheerful terms. Rejection often begins with something cheery: 'First, I must congratulate you on completing a mss. extending to more than 180,000 words.' That's fine. You feel a surge of good sensations. You have achieved something notable then? But: 'However, the text as we have it is, sadly, uncommercial.' You feel a rant coming on. How long was War and Peace for God's sake? When was length a factor in skill and success?

There is also the shiver of foreboding associated with the first word of the rejection letter. Typical unsettling words are: 'Whilst,' 'despite,' and 'disappointingly.'

Early man and woman must have known literary rejection. Violence, aggression and downright open attacks are not uncommon and they are certainly not new. Today the poet is able to supply a retort to the editor by e-mail, writing 'You know diddly-squit about good writing, you penny ha'penny hack.' But in the early times, before civilisation as we know it, in a world pre-paper and pre-written word, the editor and writer might meet at the local watering-hole:

    Editor: That crap. Take back
    Writer: You crap. Mr break neck.
    Editor: You suck.
    Writer   Get lost, dick-head.

It took several centuries for cultured discussion of aesthetic points to be aired with an objective attitude taken by both parties. Time was needed for a suitable vocabulary of rejection to be gathered and regulated. It took perhaps a century for someone to realise that a certain degree of tact and consideration was required. Medieval rebuffs were rather crude, base don Anglo-Saxon monosyllables such as ' I've pissed better poetry than this, churl!' By the great first Elizabethan age, the dialogue developed into this:

Scene; The Mermaid Tavern, London

Dramatis personae:Dick Scrote, producer/
Will Shakespeare, playwright.

DICK: Bill, the idea is fine. No problem with the
Roman bloke falling for the
Pharoah girl. Plenty of wit, sex running out
like melting ice cream, but...

WILL: Ah, there's the rub must give us pause.
From the noisy pit you want endless applause.
The words are fine, you sugar-coat it,
Then squash the struggling bard who wrote it!

DICK: Well, it's the battle of Actium, Bill. I can't see my lads putting on
A sea battle, not in my little bug-hutch. Too ambitious by far. But
The death scene with the snake – that's a cracking idea.

WILL: Fine! Then let's have five acts of dying!
Have her thinking suicide and three acts of trying.
Really, Dick, this takes the biscuit.

	I write a masterpiece and you won't risk it.
DICK:	Aye, like 'the barge she sat in burned on the water.'
	'But she wants to die and I think she ought to…'

Exit Will in a huff

WILL:	I'faith 'tis something I always expected:
	First to be prized a genius, and then rejected!

Patrons and Toadying

Traditionally, in world literature, the best way to minimise rejection was to find a patron. If the aspiring bard could find a Milord, a sovereign or at least the CEO of a great business, then the future was rosy. That is, if the bard in question could write praise with a special kind of greasiness. There were various gambits here. If the Mighty One was ugly in every respect but in his speech, say, then the thing to do was to ignore the nose as big as a shed and the bags under the eyes like sacks and the dribble from his slobbering mouth, and produce something like this:

> *Lord Butterfield excels, best in all, north, east, west and south,*
> *For he has the most glorious, silver words spilling from his mouth.*

Or, if total obsequious toadying was required (which was the case if the bard was heavily in debt and faced a spell in prison) then everything could be praised, shamefacedly, thus:

> *Bound for greatness is my Lady Farthingworth-cumber;*
> *Beauteous is she, especially in slumber;*

Though, when awake, her smile beguiles;
Men come to worship, from a hundred miles.
An epic could I pen merely upon her hair;
To be absent from her, I cannot bear.

Now, this is doggerel, but the point is that doggerel is exactly what was required. If too much talent were displayed to the would-be patron, then it could be concluded, what need was there of help?

Aspiring poets practised in front of the long mirror in the coffee house, developing the expressions of crawling, creeping and applying oleaginous words of compliment and praise. But all that was for a purpose- to please someone called a dupe, a gull, someone so thick that they would shower money on any spotty rhymer who could look artistic and pout a little.

However, in the Age of Reason, when patrons were only too happy to gather poets and writers, the poor poet had to be seen and helped at *the levee*. This was a cultural tradition designed especially to humiliate every failed, scrounging cur of a scribbler who had fallen on hard times and needed a bag of silver. The idea was that, as Milord or Milady emerged from their rooms of a morn, a line of bending, hat-tipping, slavering toadies would offer their services. It was an age of sinecures, so that Milord might think that the pathetic, fleshless, starving garret-dweller working on an epic about Roderick the Goth (see Southey, above) might do very well in the position of Hermit of the Estate. This was a wonderful position for the needy bard: he simply had to sit in a grotto on the newly improved lands of the Milord and be observed by parties of visitors. He simply had to

REJECTED

bow his head and start writing a sonnet as soon as a gaggle of culture-vultures came in sight of his den.

Yet, it is sad to relate that there were dozens if not hundreds of rejected scribes in the levees also. They were doomed to grovel and be rebuffed, as was their condition. The stories of such unwanted creative types are legion, but one stands out: the case of the poor Elizabethan poet, Thomas Bastard. Not only was he cursed with that name: he failed to be noticed after years of hard networking, then published one collection with a name that no-one could pronounce, *Chrestoleros*, in 1598. He was destined to fail, being made a Fellow at Oxford, and then having that taken away as he was charged with libel. Thomas died in a debtors' prison in 1618.

Dr Johnson, that great literary hero, was one of the first to pinpoint the source of rejection: critics. In Johnson's day, it was not too difficult to be in print. One simply wrote a poetry collection- on something scurrilous and cheeky but not actually seditious- took it to a bookseller around St. Pauls, and there you are, he would print it and give you a flat sum. There were no royalties, but that few pounds would feed you in your garret for a week or two. The booksellers were also publishers. The only problem was that lots of writers did not produce poems. Then, as now, they produced unsellable scribblings which would not attract the potential customers browsing in the old shops in between coffee-house meetings and trips down Gin Lane.

The normal unsuccessful negotiation went something like this.

Writer:	Sir, necessity compels me to offer you my sermons, written from the bottom of my heart.
Bookseller:	Necessity Sir? Why, are you hard pressed? Your attire is a trifle distressed.
Writer:	Sadly, I lost my living.
Bookseller:	Then you are technically erm... dead.
Writer:	No dear Sir, I mean I was a parson.
Bookseller:	And you wish to sell your sermons to be able to eat.
Writer:	You have it precisely.
Bookseller:	Sorry old chap. Too many sermons stuck on the shelf. We live in Godless times. People don't want to be preached at.
Writer:	Preached? Oh dear me... well I can take out the preaching and put in lots of sex and violence.
Bookseller:	How much? We'll have to change the title. I mean *One Step from Hell* will drive people away.
Writer:	What about *One Step from Hell: a guide to London's Sodom*?
Bookseller:	Fifty quid! Shake on it?

In the so-called Augustan Age – the early eighteenth century, authors became something reasonably close to what they are now: hard up, desperate and alone. But they could add that word to themselves and set up stall, or at least a desk, somewhere in a tiny attic or cellar, and work day and night. The profession of jobbing scribbler became a possibility, and we are fortunate that the diary of one such early literary man has come down to us. This is the work of Abraham Poges, epic poet and social nuisance.

Poges knew failure – and he knew it in a world in which creative talents who could not secure a leg up into society tended to sink into a Hogarthian pit of offal, rats and rejected manuscripts. He lived and slept with failure; he gnawed at the bones of rejection like some starveling pauper thrown out of the parish. He was, unknown to himself in fact, the Muse of Rejection, doomed to struggle for the crumbs of the booksellers.

Professor Sludge, the man who rescued Poges' work from oblivion, has kindly contributed this preface to the extracts from the writer's journal:

ABRAHAM POGES' BOOK
Being the journal of an Augustan scribbler

Preface
By Dr. Norbert Sludge D.Litt.

It is not often that works of literary genius come to light in today's utilitarian world, but here we have that rare thing – a true 'find'. I now know what it is to trail one's fingers nervously over the yellowing pages of an aged manuscript book – a volume unopened since the writer quit the world and all its struggles. (My partner, Geronimo, was very patient and put up with the odours). Of this now classic outpouring of Augustan literary Angst and scribbler's war very little is known, and the writer, too, is clouded in obscurity. Johnson never dined with him, nor Boswell tapped him for a loan. All we know about Poges is that he was born in obscurity, in Kent or perhaps in Cumbria or perhaps in Norfolk, and that he was rumoured to have been left to the whimsical mercies of a wet-nurse, rejected by his parents. Why, we know not. Otherwise, we know what is between these covers. I have been able to find only one reference to him in a contemporary biographical work:

> *Poges, Abraham. A tiny scribbler of trivial love verses and very pretentious epic tales in the manner of every great writer who ever lived. Wrote his first book, an epic in rhyming couplets, at the age of ten. Shunned in coffee houses by all discriminating critics. Perhaps best remembered as the power behind the actress, Jenny Jigger.'*

This is all we have, but for a scrap I have traced in a musty volume of *Notes and Queries* in which a writer of Roman tragedies wrote of Poges, ' Went t'other day to sit with Poges, and was driven from his company by the noxious stench of his body sweat. He has, I aver, not seen the inside of a bath-tub for some months, nor perhaps since he was a babe…'

I leave the reader to decide how much merit there is in this poor man's posthumous writings. All I know is that, though he will never know it, simple Poges has provided me with academic success, since that momentous day in an rotting old bookshop in a market town, I saw the battered tome and read those fateful opening words about one of his notable ailments. His body failed, as his writing did too, poor man.

Yet scholarly works have proliferated now. I append a short bibliography. Poges' works are out of print, but I hope that some smart publisher will soon remedy this.

REJECTED

*

10th. Nov. 1758

Had terrible agony with the pendulous, bulbous protrusions in my backside today. They did throb most mightily and interrupted my labour with the most sublime work of poetry the world has ever seen. I know that this time I have it – the perfect epic plot. It came to me as I wiped the grease from my collar at table. In haste I departed from the board and began a summary of the magnum opus. 'Tis to be called, *Grubbius in Oblivion* and tells the epic of an unknown, bespotted and rag-covered hack with his Hebrew of a bookseller. To win the respect and service of Tobin, a bespectacled, incestuous rogue with a passion for the flesh of insects, Grubbius has to prove worthy of the bibliophile's beauteous daughter, Wimple, and Grubbius must endure six trials of his worth. These are:

1. Hurling of the bucket of ink. Here, Grubbius has to throw, with vigour, a two-gallon pail of ink across a wide chasm without one spot of liquid settling on an amused crowd of clergymen in white surplices at the valley bottom. The hero trains by drinking strong ale and abstaining from commerce with nought but lads for seven weeks together. (Seven being a magick number, Grubbius having seven nipples it was said). At the end of the trial, the Yorkshire sleep close to the chasm do suffer mightily after Grubbius' ascetic life.
2. Going without gin for a week. A most gruelling demand. He sweats like a pigge.

3. The attendance at St. Agrippa's school as usher for a term. In which our hero is waylaid by sundry unruly scholars.
4. The cleansing of Lord Gout's stables. The classical theme will make me out a scholar. In which Grubbius allows the waters of the cesspool to free the stables of clotted dung, yet the foule stinke thereof does wax most terrible noxious to the snout and orbs.
5. The duel with Sir Jittering Crimp. In which G. receives some ventilation of an bigge-bone in the leg due to the rapid passing-through thereof of a massy agglomeration of buckshot metals.
6. The final labour is, to Wimple, the Lady of the Becke, most dear. Here G. must ope the door to her chamber using nought but his wide and sturdy shoulders. The door is passing thicke and severe bruises are sustained yet G. lives on, unable to gratify his carnal desires for some months. What think ye, reader of time to come? Am I vain? Do I suffer from the vanity of fine writers? God bless the mark!

On the morrow I take my great plan to Jacob in St.Paul's Churchyard. 'Tis worthy of a guinea and so to do a few hours in the coffee house and mayhap the purchase of a wench. A thought enters my pate – is not Grubbius something of myself? Yea great Milton writ 'On his blindness' – then why not Abe Poges in like manner reveal himself?

By the by, young Jenny at the druggists would not yield – again. The little bauble plays coy with me. That small closet behind the shelf is most suitable for the seduction, yet she EVEN

NOW will not be cajoled. Egad, I still have mine own hair and teeth and not turned forty years and two yet! Does the maid abhor me? 'Tis my perfume mayhap. Too much rubbed around my wet member? I must try the fortress yet again – this time with more compendious strength in the army. I shall have her and be content.

Mayhap 'tis the smell of my hands. I have a particular essence dwelling there that art and craft cannot remove. How many time shave I essayed the use of potions and unguents to shift that stench. Yet it will persist. My sister, Wrestling Soul Poges, accounts it to my youthful habit of avoiding clean water.

Addendum: Not to forget to call in at Rayworth's Chocolate House as that foul Johnson is guaranteed not to be there. Whenever he spies me, the great bulk never misses the opportunity of railing and teasing at me for the farce of my one theatrical work. I wish he would choke on his steak -–and by God, why can't he stop his face from twitching? In his company, I will start to twitch also, in counterpoint. I suppose he was quite good once – after all, he did write that tedious dictionary.

11th November

The manuscript was completed this day but hell followed. Ye Gods! Today was the worst day of my life. Delays and tribulations pursue me like a pack of hungry curs chasing the fox. I am a hunted man and fate is in pursuit. Did Genius ever bear such pangs? The day began ill, when I spewed mightily upon rising from bed, and my pate overhung the tub for close on one hour. My good landlady, Mrs. Turtle, did wax most satirical. She did aver that filling my maw with Muscadel and delicacies was the cause. Yet surely a man – a literary man to boot – needs the sensual gratification of a good piece of hoggery from time to time. Nothing tempts the lips more than a slice of seed cake or a joint of lamb.

Well, there was I in my nethers when Mrs. Turtle 'gins to snigger most rudely at my plight. I was owing three weeks' rent, else she would have received a bowl of piss in her visage.

Worse was to come, for on sitting at my desk, I discovered that the papers on which I writ my Epic Prologue had vanished. Imagine my plight. This was the opus which was to take my name into every literary weekly in the City, and in had gone. Mrs. Turtle vowed she had not lighted the fire with them, and so a search began, and egad, if the cat had not taken them to have her kitlings on! So Mrs. Turtle claimed. The tabby whore has been with kitling for two dozen times, I swear. The sides of nature will not sustain it, as the Bard says.

There was the bloody sludge and the squealing things mewling most piteously. My heart would have gone soft is 'twere not for the huge difficulty in distinguishing the letters of my masterpiece that lay beneath, besmirched.

13th November

By Saint Hugh, the great work was copied out again, and finally delivered to the bookseller. He'll see its genius at once. He cannot resist my words, the exquisite form, the sublime rhyming…This is my time. The world will see me for the genius I am. No long will my bushel be under the light, or my light under the bushel. (Note to self: what is a bushel?)

14th November

The manuscript was returned. I say that boldly, like a man. But inwardly I weep like a scolded child. The bookseller's lad delivered it, and sniggered as he threw it into my cellar.

May all publishers and their minions die slowly, of the plague!

*

Hacks like Poges infested the East End, and many had the fate of chewing on leather and going raving mad after finding that their sermons or their huge epic poems were 'not commercial.'

As time went on, and writing became more sophisticated, writing was seen as a branch of mental derangement, as Robert Burton, the specialist in insanity, knew, and he put it simply: 'All poets are mad.' Shakespeare, in *A Midsummer Night's Dream,* agreed:

> *The lunatic, the lover and the poet,*
> *Are of imagination all compact.'*

However, sympathy in this respect was rare indeed. There is no record of a publisher ever saying to his colleagues, 'Whatever you do, don't reject poor Tom Toddle's work… he'll top himself!'

The professionalization of rejection took a long time to mature. This is a rough summary of how the language and attitudes developed and changed:

BEFORE REJECTION SLIPS

Dark Ages:	Your poem is shit.
Medieval:	Poor stuff. Go be a ploughman
Tudor:	Write that again and I'll cut your hand off.
Stuart:	Say the king is great and I'll reconsider
Augustan	Inferior drivel, old man. Light the fire with it.
Georgian:	The divel take it, I won't!
Victorian:	We most reluctantly decline to accept your manuscript.
Twentieth Century:	Not this time, Mr Smith.
Contemporary:	Sadly, this does not fit with our current lists, go brand yourself.

In the time of wigs, duels and fifteen-course dinners, those in search of patrons were not always poetasters, pretenders and tender wilting souls. Take Jean-Louis De Lolme for instance. He is the author of a standard work on British politics: *Constitution of England*. This finally found print in 1771 and is now recognised as a classic work on the English political system and liberty, with an analysis of the Separation of Powers. But poor De Lolme was widely rebuffed. As Isaac D'Israeli, father of the Prime Minister Benjamin, wrote of this struggling author:

> *'The fact is mortifying to record, that the author who wanted every aid, received less encouragement than if he had solicited subscription for a raving novel or an idle poem. De Lolme was compelled to traffic with booksellers for this work; and as he was a theoretical rather than a practical politician, he was a bad trader...He lived... in extreme poverty and decay... He never appears to have received a solitary atten-*

tion, and became so disgusted with authorship that he preferred silently to endure its poverty rather than its vexations.'

Still, after using the subscription method, his great work finally saw print.

Even Dr Johnson had problems with his patron, Lord Chesterfield. Johnson planned to write his great *Dictionary of the English Language* (1755) using no more than his own efforts and a team of scribes, working in his attic off Fleet Street. Chesterfield promised much but tended to forget and Johnson was never in his mind, other than receiving a payment of ten pounds. The result was that, as the magnum opus was completed, he wrote to Chesterfield, stating that: 'Is not a patron, my Lord, one who looks with unconcern on a man struggling for life in the water, and when he has reached ground, encumbers him with help?' Consequently, the definition of a patron in the great dictionary was: ' One who countenances, supports or protects. Commonly a wretch who supports with insolence, and is paid with flattery.'

Rejection Escalates

Some writers were above criticism of course, and so they could never know the emotional volcano of rejection. A classic example is Napoleon Bonaparte, who was an author as well as an Emperor. Not only did he write his memoirs, but as a young man he published a novella, *Clisson et Eugenie*, a story of love and war. This was in 1795, when other scribes such as Wordsworth and Coleridge were testing the water with their new lyrics. Napoleon went for the full Monty in Romantic terms, with idyllic country life and the trials of war. No-one said to Boney,

'Much as we admire your work, we feel unable to publish...' No, the Bastille would have awaited that poor editor with a hatchet job to do.

Of course, rejection letters became more common in the late Victorian period, when such matters as copyright and author-publisher relations were revolutionised. The Society of Authors was created, and gradually the profession of author became more accepted rather than seen as some kind of wayward aberration undertaken often by younger sons who wanted to avoid the law or the army or the church.

In 1896, Arnold Bennett sent his first novel, *A Man from the North* to publisher John Lane. The response was favourable, but strangely, with a very negative comment: 'He had no fault whatever to find with the novel *qua* novel, but he said it would probably not be popular.' Bennett wrote in his journal. But 'I will publish it' said Lane and Bennett said merely 'That is very good of you.' The point is that reasons were given

In the usual situation of the aspiring scribe and the publisher, there is no time for reasons other than such platitudes as ' Not at this time' or 'Our lists are full' or 'We advise you to read the *Writers and Artists Yearbook*. '

From the early nineteenth century, as authorship became both more common and more attainable, one's *nom de plume* became important and a bad name would easily become a problem. The Russian poet, Anna Akhmatova, ended up with that name because her father thought that if she printed her real family name – Gorenko- it would bring disgrace on him and his own, particularly, as Joseph Brodsky has pointed out, the Gorenkos were posh and actually lived in the same village as the Tsar (his *dacha*, or country home): Tsarskoe Selo.

But in modern times, one's writing name is so important that it may well be a factor determining acceptance rather than rejection. Conversely, names have to be relevant to the genre in question. A thriller writer called John Smith may be well advised to transmute into Jake Delaney or Hank Belmoth.

When the literary agents arrived, and there were business meetings and lunches, with the poor author either invited to be inspected or left at home to await the decision, rejections were often more long-winded. But in the end, the poor scribe's fate lay in the balance and Grub Street was and still is a precarious place. If we look for a writer whose life and career illustrates the struggles of the writer to be heard and promoted, published and reviewed, arguably George Gissing is the template. He worked extremely hard, but as a young man he had someone even better than a patron- and influential friend already in the heart of literary networks around London. This was Fredric Harrison, and as Paul Delany wrote in his biography of Gissing, Harrison '… wrote to five editors of reviews, and other influential figures of his acquaintance' to help Gissing be known and his work circulated.

Of course, there is another form of rejection, and this is primarily known in the world of the dramatist. This is the language of rotten tomatoes and cat-calls, booing and heckling. In the eighteenth century and the regency in particular, drama was so popular for all classes and types that stage managers and impresarios would give anything a try, such was their creative courage (or lust for profit). The failures are legion, and accounts of the noisy rejection of a piece by the mob make sad reading.

One such spectacular criticism was made by the audience in 1814 when one writer's short drama, *The Forest of Bondii* was presented, and in this a dog was to be on stage. There was a contractual disagreement by the men in suits and the piece was never presented, but substituted. A riot followed. As to the author, his play was written, contracted and never performed.

On the other hand, we have to feel sympathy for the author W H C Nation, who wrote a pantomime, *Red Riding Hood,* which played to an audience of two. These brave souls would not budge from the upper circle, and so the stalls were bare, and the performers suffered the fate of having to follow the old rule that the show must go on. As for Mr Nation, maybe he wept in the green room.

Performance also brings the most direct censure and rebuttal of all: physical contact. In 1949 the poet, Stephen Spender, was giving a reading of his work in the crypt of the Ethical Church in Bayswater, when the South African poet, Roy Campbell, struggled on stage, and took a swing at the poet, cracking him on the nose. Campbell escaped the long arm of the law; Spender was very tolerant and understanding, writing later that he was hit 'with an honest sergeant's fist.' One thing is certain though: the author was in no doubt about the listener's opinion: no doubt there. It was a refreshing change from the doubletalk of literary criticism, we might suggest.

Overall, rejection of authors has been a textless history: we are talking letters and notes made for the rejection bin. Who would want to keep them anyway, and be constantly reminded of failure?

REJECTED

The paper chase of letters and rejection slips may just be possible, but what if the rebuff comes from a relative? Vera Brittain suffered this, when her husband, George Catlin, did not like the manuscript of the future modern classic, *Testament of Youth*. As Mark Bostridge explained in an introduction to Brittain's work: ' Catlin scrawled his comments in the margins of the typescript: 'intolerable', 'pretty terrible' – believing that his wife's book would hold him up to ridicule among his academic colleagues…'

5

SELF-PUBLISHERS AND SELF-PROMOTERS

Of course, there has always been one way of preventing rejection. That is to publish one's own work, and even better, to write the reviews of the book oneself. Of course, in 2013, anyone may easily publish their e-book and say that they are a successful author – and so they are, according to the lowest of several definitions of 'published.'

This is not a new trend, as recent revelations of such vanity trips being done on Amazon Books pages. Of course, self-publishing is now an industry open to all. But there are notable examples of very famous authors making sure that reviews were favourable. Walt Whitman, for instance, poet of *The Leaves of Grass* (1855) not only self-published that great, momentous work of American literature: he also wrote some good reviews. He wrote, of his own book, 'Walt Whitman's method in the construction of his songs is strictly the method of Italian opera, which when heard, confounds the new person aforesaid....impresses him as if all the sounds of earth and hell were tumbled promiscuously together.'

This little ego-trip is of course all a part of a marketing strategy, and is not exactly a major transgression; yet history shows us that rebuffs by the great and powerful inflicted on the little minnows of the publishing world, the authors, generates some grand stories. One of the most intriguing is the tale of Josef Goebbels' failure as a writer. He took a Ph.D. in Drama at the University of Heidelberg; he then wrote some plays and a novel called *Michael* which nobody wanted. He also wrote several pieces for the newspapers but was rejected there too.

Goebbels set off for Berlin, where Hitler was to make him *Gauleiter*, with his typescript of his novel in a bag. Let's imagine that journey.

Ankles and Smiles
A story of 1928

The little man clung to his suitcase, hands clamped on the clasp. It was all he had, heading for this new life in the big city. The important letter was in there, and his photos, his journal, and manuscript of *Michael Voorman*. That novel was going to make his name. Too long he had been alone. Too long the coldness of the world had shunned him. His genius would soon be known. Those two strangers there – they would soon know what power was in him, deep in him, waiting to burst out into an immense love, a passion too strong to contain.

In his mind's eye he saw the letter in the case: an important letter, from an important man, giving him an introduction to the centre of things – the great city of Frederick the Great. He thought of himself walking down to Ku-Damm and sitting in the great cafes where you could see images of the Vienna Woods or the tableau of a storm in the Black Forest. He had read and dreamed of the city, and its beauty, its charm.

It had been a long, tiring journey and great stretches of Germany had filled the vista from the carriage window for what seemed like days. How grim it all was, he thought, how damned dead, in need of a great stream of colour through its black tissue. There was a chill in the air, and the train was not well heated. The three people in the carriage were huddled into their coats: the girl in her fur, the old man in his black barathea, and the little, dark man squat in the corner away from the light of the window seemed under-dressed for the season.

The little man had wanted to speak since they left Frankfurt, but decided to read his book instead. But his eyes and his thoughts were completely on the girl. What was she – nineteen? Was that her father with her, he wondered. They spoke occasionally, so they obviously knew each other, but there was no evidence of any warmth between them. But how he relished those little feminine details: the strand of hair falling down her neck, and the blue eyes, like little heavens. She was exquisite.

He imagined himself kissing that little round cheek, with its touch of natural ruddy life: no need of rouge there. Why, she was untouched. He had always longed for virgins, always written his poems about them, pursued them, adored them. Young, fair-haired, gentle girls from the provinces. They were the soul of the feminine in the world – its quintessence.

He smiled at her. She looked away. She was an exciting woman. He would put her into his novel when next he sat down to work on it.

He thought about his suitcase again, and about his novel. It was now almost epic in scale, with all the essence of his young life distilled there into a poetic, intense work that would make Germany sit up and think again about art, about the powerful impulses of success and achievement. These two strangers had no idea what was in that small brown suitcase.

"Now, Marta, where is my handkerchief? I'm feeling a touch ill." The chubby old man shuffled restlessly in his seat. The girl looked in her bag and produced an embroidered, very dainty hanky for him.

"Here my love, do keep cool – have some water. I have some in the bottle still."

The little man's heart stirred with the excitement of the word 'love' from her lips. It was like some wild awakening in his hungry spirit. He felt like a starving animal out in the winter snow, struggling from window to window of the human dwellings, shut out, shut out from love. And as he sneaked a look at her he saw, just as she leaned across, her ankle, as her long skirt lifted slightly. His glance caught a white sock and a few inches of flesh above. So delicate, so maidenly. He felt his desire to kiss her neck or her ankle, and the heat at his crotch, the writhing of his lust, made him ashamed.

"Sir, would you care for a little water?"

She was speaking to him. He had to rouse all his consciousness to answer her, as in his mind he saw her naked. "Why, you are so kind, and yes, I would love some."

"Hot hey? July– not far from Berlin – bound to be warm. A bohemian place I hear?" The old man was trying to be civil.

"Yes, yes… I suppose so. Deliciously decadent I hear. We're nearly there now."

"About twenty miles from Berlin I'd say. I'm Kurt Neschlin by the way, and this is my niece, Marta, on our way to my brother – he has a business in the city."

He looked as if to ask the little man's name, but at that moment, the train lurched to a halt and the girl was thrown across towards the little man, and his suitcase fell onto the floor, spilling its contents into all corners.

"Oh my God! My things… my precious things… I must get them all back in here." The little man scrambled around the floor, and the man and girl moved their legs aside for him to look. One by one he retrieved the items. His hands searched the dark crannies under the seats, finding cobwebs and broken pencils. But his eyes saw the delicious ankle of the girl again, and he was so close to the white sock and the band of exposed flesh that he felt the urge to kiss, and it was too strong. His body shook with a mixture of fear and excitement. He sensed his head move forward slowly and his lips purse, inching closer. Then the wonderful shiver of bliss as he gently kissed the skin.

The girl did not move and made no noise. There was no reaction, except, when the little man sat up again, checking his suitcase, he saw her face, now bright red with embarrassment. "Excuse me for prying, but I see that you are a writer… a poet!" The old man said, nodding towards an open notebook in the middle of the floor. It was obviously a poetic text, across the page, in a bold, scholarly hand.

But the little man was shaking. He was trembling with desire. The girl was looking away, out of the window, to hide her astonishment. She may have been crying, the little man sensed. Or did she feel the exquisite tremor of love as well?

"Yes, I am a writer – I write poetry and fiction. I have been a student for many years. I am going to Berlin to try to achieve something."

"But you have achieved something – you have quite clearly filled this large notebook, my young friend." The old man sneezed then, and Marta, now recovered from her shock, took his cup before it spilled.

The bits and pieces were now all gathered up, and they were carefully checked. He spoke to himself as he listed them. "Diary, pen, clock, erm… letter. The letter is not there!"

"Do you mean to be published? Is that why you go to Berlin young man?" The old man asked, but the little man's thoughts were on the missing letter. "If you do – why, that is my brother's business!"

"What? He is a publisher – of fiction?"

"Why yes, see what a fortuitous meeting this is, my student friend. Perhaps I could introduce you…"

At that second, Marta stepped in. "No uncle. No…"

Her tone was very firm, almost angry and aggressive.

"What do you mean my dear… this young man is underfed and under-clothed… look at him, he needs a square meal. No doubt he has been creating a masterpiece in an attic for years – he is to be the next great poet!"

She could not find words to answer the point. But her hand was shaking as she held her cup and her uncle noticed this. "My dear, are you upset in some way? Are you feeling quite well?"

The little man was on the floor again, smiling with uneasiness. "The letter… it *has* to be here."

This time, the girl walked to the door, well away from him. The old man stood up and went to her. The letter was, in fact, on a seat, and she picked it up. There was a photograph of the young man. He looked Mediterranean, she thought, like an Italian or a Greek, but then she saw the name. It was definitely a German name.

"Ah, you have it… thank you Miss." He snatched it from her. His smile showed his strong teeth, and the tired eyes expressed a certain desperation, but for a second, their hands touched, and she felt a loneliness, a longing in him.

"I really didn't mean to make a fuss… just that I have no… no copies you see."

They sat down again. An official came into the carriage. "Berlin in five minutes…please check you do not leave anything on the train, good people. Thank you for your co-operation."

"So, are you going to meet us in Berlin young man, and meet my brother? He will look at your work, I'm sure. He's always looking for new talent. All the world is reading, I think.'

"What is his name?"

"Hessler."

"Oh, I see." The little man's head dropped in dismay. "He has already, how shall I say, *rejected* my work."

There was a long silence, before Marta said, "Mr Goebbels, I see you have a job to go to… I could not help reading your letter. What is a Gauleiter?"

The old man was going to explain, but was muddled. His face showed a shadow of concern, as a cloud passes over a lawn on a summer day.

"It means I take charge… of a certain company, you might say."

"A businessman then?" Marta asked.

"Yes, I'm in business."

"What's your company young man?" The old man asked, politely.

"They make stationery… pens and inkwells and typing equipment… and so on."

The little man smiled. He could say no more without ruining his chances of arranging a meeting with the publisher. He was about to press the point with the old man, angling for a meeting with his powerful brother, when, with the sway of the train, a handgun slid out from under a seat. Without thinking, the little man picked it up. "Good God! I forgot this!"

Scarcely had he said the words when he realised what he had done. He looked up and his gaze met their eyes. In a matter of seconds, they were out of the carriage and into the corridor, the old man ushering his niece to safety. He seemed to dart glances in all directions, as if expecting something he couldn't handle.

'Checking papers, they're checking papers again, *liebschen*. Keep close to me.'

In minutes, the train pulled into Berlin. The noise engulfed all attempts at talk. The old man clutched his suitcase as if it were solid gold. A man needed two brains and a dozen hands in this city, he thought to himself.

The little man stood alone in the carriage, watching them walk into the crowd. He willed her to turn and look at him, his mind commanding her to look back before she walked into the anonymous city crowd. Further and further they went. But he stared and willed her. She would. She would turn to him. Everything would be lost if she walked on, unmoved.
Marta Neschlin, look at me… never forget me…
The face turned to him. He just made out a smile. It didn't matter to the little man whether it was a smile of love or fear.

Subscribers please!

In the eighteenth century there emerged the notion of subscription. This meant that there was a new version of failure. The poor aspiring author acquired someone powerful in the literary world, presented his or her gems of imagination, and was told that publishing would be possible – as long as the poor hack could find a certain number of subscribers. These were people who, in signing up as subscribers, agreed to buy a copy of the work when it was printed. One of the most prolonged and well documented examples of this is in the life of Northamptonshire poet, John Clare.

Clare was a country labourer, drifting across a number of varieties of casual labour; he realized that he had a capacity for versifying and singing, and when he read the massive eighteenth century best-seller, James Thomson's poems of nature, *The Seasons*, he was inspired to write himself. He scraped together money to buy a notebook and started to write manuscript drafts of his poems after he composed them during a working day. Then came the notion of publication.

He was taken up by a Stamford bookseller, who offered subscription as a way into print; the problem was that the first step was to gather over a hundred subscribers. Clare did quite well in that, but the printer was charging him money also. Only when he came across a young, more supportive printer called Ned Drury did things start to happen. Drury saw that other 'peasant poets' such as Burns, Bloomfield and Kirke White, had succeeded. Soon the local gentry were involved and the first collection. Opinions were sought from various educated men, and some were discouraging, such as the response of a vicar called Twopenny, who, after reading some Clare poems, according to Jonathan Bate, 'Sent them back with a cold note stating that he had no objection to assist in raising the poor man a small subscription, though the poems appeared to him to possess no merit to be worthy of publication.' But eventually, *Poems Descriptive of Rural Life and Scenery* was in print, published by Taylor and Hessey, in 1820.

Subscription may have been an invitation to fail, if the hapless poet could not access a wide and supportive social circle. But in the high Victorian years, as provincial publishing and writing expanded, it became a viable option. The shelves of antiquarian bookshops are well stocked with elaborately produced, often very beautiful anthologies of poetry from this period, with a list of subscribers at the back of the book. One significant volume in this format is worth a special mention though: *Poets of Keighley, Bingley and Howarth* (1891), edited by a moustachioed dentist-poet from Bradford called Charles F Forshaw, contains, alongside such gems as 'Saxon Grit' by the Rev. Robert Collyer, ten poems by members of the Bronte family. The book appeared because almost 250 subscribers gave their name. A definite bonus of subscribing, however, was the opportunity of a 'plug' – so that, for example, we learn that Matthew Harman was the author of *Poetic Buds*.

Today, in contrast, we have a similar concept still alive and well: the term is 'crowd-funding' which seems to mean that the author finds a celebrity and then tries to sign up lots of fans of the said celebrity, to buy the author's book when ready. Justin Pollard has written about this in *The Author*, the magazine of the Society of Authors. He approached Terry Jones (the Monty Python star) and everything appears to have worked well. But Justin Pollard concludes: ' A growing number of authors... are now discovering that crowd-funding provides a chance to build a direct and lasting relationship with their most loyal audience.' It sounds like true love.

Printing by subscription has been remarkably successful, and in the case of Robert Burns, it was his real 'launch.' In July, 1786, his volume, *Poems Chiefly in the Scottish Dialect* was published in Kilmarnock. Over 600 copies were printed, and in three weeks, all but thirteen were sold. A few drams were downed in the hostelry that night, after the figures were added up. It seems that Rabbie had very little trouble finding supporters: he won over those who counted, and who had networks already, and the rest is history.

REJECTED

Shooting Yourself in the Pen-Hand

Being the source of your own failure is not too difficult. There are few aspects of the literary life as common and often inevitable, as the setback caused by the writer's own daftness. In my writing trajectory I have been responsible for dozens of my failures. As a breed, one of our common faults is not having sufficient self-belief.

The self-inflicted rejection inevitably follows. Writers and artists are famously fussy, inveterate critics of their own work. An apochryphal story told of James Joyce illustrates this. One day he met a friend who asked how the new book was going? 'Very well indeed,' said Joyce, ' I did a sentence today!' He had written one sentence that he was contented with. There may have been two hundred others written and then erased.

This self-editing and self-criticism is the deepest, most complex variety of rejection. It originates in the profound notion that before the written word appears on the page, there is a pre-verbal idea, image or feeling in the writer's brain. The task then is how to get that precise pre-verbal 'thing' inside out onto the page in the exact form in which it exists inside the head. Hence the phenomenon of 'drafts' and of 'versions.' A case in point is William Wordsworth's great enterprise he called *The Recluse*. This was a massive concept, based on a full account of the growth of a poet's mind. The first phase of this was the long poem, *The Prelude*. He started work on this around 1798, and that draft was eventually in print by 1805; after that it was refashioned, Wordsworth repeatedly messing with it, re-thinking it, until the final version was published in 1850, after the poet's death.

SELF-PUBLISHERS AND SELF-PROMOTERS

All this introduces the question: how best to try to avoid rejection? Well, maybe the answer is to do one's best to be the kind of writer who has the right stock of knowledge for a start. The critic James Agate had some thoughts about this back in the 1930s.

We need to think again about James Agate. His books lie unexplored on dusty shelves, and in fact he achieved something magnificent- something extremely rare in autobiography- and what he did and why is something that is urgently needed in today's situation regarding the centrality of words in one's creative life.

He was born in 1877 near Salford, and began his career in journalism in 1907. His mother had French ancestry and a love of music, and James soon absorbed European influences in his own aesthetics; as he advanced in drama reviewing his circle of friends expanded, and included Shaw, Beerbohm and Ivor Brown. The short essay was arguably his natural form, as he was skilled in writing the kind of Humour from everyday life that Charles Lamb' work illustrated for him. Then came his decision to put his own routines, pleasures and thinking at the heart of his work.

In the course of writing his massive diary, *Ego*, the drama critic and all-round bookman did a word-count of production: ' In the vulgar scale of quantity I have in the last fifteen years re-invested 3,860,000 words. Roughly, four-fifths of *The Human Comedy*, which took Balzac eighteen years...' He had decided to the start the work in the 30s after having already established himself as a critic and essayist. His novels did not succeed in the same way as his discursive prose, and little of his work is now in print. Yet his diary affirms one remarkable aspect of writing when it works: the ability of one's words to invite others to share in the microcosm that is yourself. Not only did Agate spin out his words, mainly for *Sunday Times*, *Express* and *Manchester Guardian*, but he relished the challenge of being that rare breed, the literary man of culture whose invitation to readers to share his tastes and preoccupations, and actually make that place welcoming.

His world as a jobbing writer and rather Pepysian character consisted of more or less the same material through his life: Sarah Bernhardt, French literature, cricket, golf, show ponies and the theatre. In the interstices of that edifice there were factors such as constant debt, travels across Britain, endless letters on topics from philosophy to old books. In the midst of his great work, he asked himself: 'Why am I keeping this diary? Answer: because it is part of the insane desire to perpetuate oneself.' He had, by around 1934, written so much to order, or for income, that the time had come to write what he wanted. Although he still recorded such details as the fact that he had sold a book to a publisher for a few hundred pounds, what really mattered was that there were 'lots of things I want to say that other writers put into novels and accepted essayists put into essays.'

Agate's diary is a huge room cluttered by insistent arguments for quality in art, criticism of what is not up to the mark, reminders of his markers of excellence –favourite actors, his best ponies, W G Grace and Charles Lamb for instance – and of course, explanations of his ongoing chaos regarding money. His cash went on classy hotels, motoring, good wine, and in fact everything that Oscar Wilde would have approved of. He explained to his faithful readers who shared in his enterprise that he would not talk about his sex life, explaining that he had married when young and then left heterosexual life behind him. One paragraph is all we have, and my own reflection of *how refreshing to get that out of the way* is, admittedly, bizarre in our world of prurient, trivialising interest in other's private lives.

His world may seem elitist, as he loves to quote from other languages, show off his wide reading, and pass dogmatic judgements. But these are Johnsonian habits, out to provoke. To fully enter his room and share his thoughts, there is an entrance exam. In January 1946 he explains the required knowledge, after meeting 'a Bloomsburyite who started babbling about Jean-Paul Sartre' who 'in the course of his babbling let out that he had never heard of Fred Karno.' Hence we have Agate's 'General Knowledge paper for a Youth Envisaging a Literary Career.' This comes from Agate's reflection on what the 'mooncalf' did not know, such as:

> *He thought the earth's diameter was 93,000 miles… Hadn't heard of Euclid… Had never read a word of Milton, Tennyson, Keats. Couldn't quote any line from Gray's Elegy. Couldn't fill in the blanks in 'From fairest…… creatures we desire increase' Saw nothing wrong about 'The expensive spirit is a waste of shame….didn't know what school Tom Brown went to or who was its headmaster. Thought Henry VIII had eight wives…'*

On reading this, I suddenly felt inadequate (and I have three degrees in literary studies). I have relished sharing his reflections on taste, aesthetics and horses, but when I read this, I still felt rather like the Bloomsburyite. But his entrance paper is not, in spite of the tone, meant to be snobbish. Agate assumed, again like Johnson, that life was to be taken in huge gulps, and that reading as well as fine dining or buying furniture should be fully acquired and understood, and that there was a common cultural heritage we should all know so that we communicate fully. The only problem is about what is on his curriculum.

Moreover, this passage in *Ego* set me thinking. If we had one, what would the entrance paper for 2013 be? Is there a similar curriculum that we acquire through a mix of school, conversation and reading? Our age of information overload forces on us the skills of multi-tasking, slavery to gadgets and a questionable reliance on Wikipedia. Agate would have detested any knowledge taken in sound bites or from a 'quick read' habit.

As he was reaching the end of his vast autobiographical undertaking, Agate had the odd experience of reading his own obituary. His friend Alan Dent, waiting for him in a restaurant, was writing the obituary for *The Manchester Guardian*, and as Agate was late, he began writing the piece at the corner table. But Agate arrived, understood the situation and said, 'Come boy –as one journalist to another- let me read what you really think of me!'

The last diary entry was made on 2 June, 1947. Four days later, as Dent wrote, ' He had a heart attack, collapsed and died beside his bed.' Beneath the apparent opinionated, prejudicial and cogent expressions of his likes and dislikes, and of success and failure, there was a poet. This part of him existed in the mess and worry of everyday life, with its deadlines, its second-class fare and its insistence on plaguing him with bills and final demands. In one long section of the diary, he wrote a sequence of paragraphs describing some of the glorious moments in his life. These begin with: 'Of early days at Old Trafford,' 'Of being taken to see Toole and finding him unfunny,' and 'Of driving from Chapel-en-le-Frith to Disley on Sunday evenings to dine and argue with Edgar Baerlein...'

If the reader stays with him over the course of nine solid volumes of *Ego*, then the invitation to Agate's world will offer deep rewards, things far more than encounters with forgotten plays and arguments about actors or cricketers: the real pleasure is in sharing what is today a very rare indulgence. That consist of treading among the mental clutter of a discerning, educated mind being allowed by a publisher to write about anything at any time, in any place, and not worry about writing something that will maintain his 'brand' or wander away from established genre conventions.

Yet we still have the subject of the entrance paper. I ask myself: for today's cultural and literary acquisitions for ' a youth envisaging a literary career.' When I was twenty I thought that stacking up lots of facts would help me as a writer. It did and it didn't. The jury is out. But as far as Agate was concerned, his in-depth education certainly helped him into print. He had about fifty volumes to his name as he exited this life for the next 'stage.'

Agate reminded everyone that being a writer is not a soft option. Too much naïve vanity is, he insisted a sure recipe for falling on one's face.

Maybe, in 2013, all we can say for sure is that researching one's own 'patch' of knowledge, as a basis for writing, can't be a bad thing. It served Bernard Cornwell very well indeed in his conception of the Sharpe novels.

Finally, there is the question of a writer being half-rejected. That is, the dreaded problem of the re-write. This is when the publisher's letter is a rejection of what has been submitted, but their door is left open, as it were. The wording goes something like this: 'Despite these misgivings, we feel that, with considerable effort tin re-writing the first six chapters, there may be a possibility that your novel may be reconsidered…'

When the writer him or herself wants to rewrite- to change the genre or the voice, there is a challenge ahead. I'd like to imagine a scene from the life of such a writer, let us call him something very individual and odd: Schofield Mobyn.

A Chapter of Errors

James Slayne (publisher)

Schofield Mobyn   (writer and postman)

A knock
Slayne, rough and direct, calls sharply:
SLAYNE: Come in
MOBYN: Good morning Mr Slayne. Sunny today.
SLAYNE: Ah yes… come in Hank. It's really good to see you after so long. Come on in. I loved *Cactus Gulch* by the way- when's the next one ready?
MOBYN: Well, er…
SLAYNE: Now then, don't hide your light under a bushel. After ten Slim Gillray Books, you've a right to some confidence, surely! I mean, your readers

	Don't know you're a postman in Clapham do they? Thank God!
MOBYN:	Actually, I'm changing. That is... I've changed.
SLAYNE:	What? Oh course you have, joke see!
MOBYN:	Really... I can see that you haven't read the manuscript I sent you.
SLAYNE:	What? I didn't know you'd sent one.
MOBYN:	Oh well, there must be a mix-up.
SLAYNE:	It must be in the wrong file.. I'll get Jack to search for it.
MOBYN:	No, don't bother. I could explain.
SLAYNE:	What do you mean- explain?
MOBYN:	Well, in the new story, I'm breaking new ground.
SLAYNE:	(suspiciously) How do you mean exactly?
MOBYN:	You see, Slim Gillray, he's changed.
SLAYNE:	Changed? How do you mean? You mean he maybe has silver guns now?
MOBYN:	No. Changed ever so little
SLAYNE:	In what way? Tell me, Schofield!
MOBYN:	Well, he reads books and he...
SLAYNE:	Reads a book! Hell, no... Slim Gillray?
MOBYN:	Yes, I thought it was time he had other interests. An intellectual side to him, like.
SLAYNE:	Intellectual! My God! Schofield, what are you telling me? We are talking about Slim Gillray, the guy who split Red Pony's skull with an axe! Slim Gillray is the geyser who makes the Sioux shit

themselves with bloody fear when he so much as lights a fag.

This cowboy, let me remind you, shaves with a Bowie knife and makes John Wayne look like an accounts clerk. Schofield, does this seem like a bloody intellectual to you? Does it?

PAUSE

MOBYN: Not exactly.

SLAYNE: Not exactly! On me old lady's grave, I swear I've never had any bloke in this room before who's such a weird idea of the punters' tastes. Your readers, Mr Mobyn, are waiting for Slim to get even with that bandido git… what's his name, Manfred?

MOBYN: You refer to Alfredo Mendoza, the Scourge of the Long Knives

SLAYNE: Exactly. Your loyal readers, Mobyn, are waitin' for Slim To get even with the sombrero-totin' swine. What's he Gonna do now- discuss Bertrand Russell with him?

MOBYN: Not really, Mr Slayne.

SLAYNE: Tell me Mobyn, why did you write the Slim Gillray books in the first place?

MOBYN: Well, I always enjoyed the classics.

SLAYNE: Crap! Greenbacks, Mobyn. You did it for the bread!

MOBYN: (*Schoolmaster's tone now*)

In a way, yes. But there was more to it. I always felt, because Of my grammar school education, that literature should amuse AND instruct. Great writing should lead the reader into those experiences that he himself will never perceive...

SLAYNE: You mean experiences like gunning down three commancheros And riding on a bronco upside-down?

MOBYN: Not exactly that.

SLAYNE: I suppose Hamlet went hunting sharks did he? And what about Dickens's Pip O'Neal, gunslinger of Fleet Street?

MOBYN: I think I detect a hint of sarcasm in your tone Mr Slayne

SLAYNE: You think right me old china. A great dollop of sarcasm.
I mean for instance, did Schofield Mobyn, postman and stamp collector become Hank Coogan? Or Shakespeare call himself
Wild Bill Shakes, the sun slinger with DTs?

MOBYN: I feel that we have drifted a little from the topic in hand.

SLAYNE: The topic in hand, Mobyn, is that I will not publish your book-
What's it called?

MOBYN: *Slim Goes to College*

SLAYNE: What?

MOBYN: I toyed with *Slim Majors in Hegelian Philosophy* but that sounded pretentious.

SLAYNE: Dead right. Look, go home again, write me a plain tale of Saloon women and brutal murders and I'll forgive this lapse. Let's be frank –your identity as Hank Coogan has made me A packet. Since Slim first shot a hole in Big Tex, this firm has just blossomed, so please, don't spoil our Slim, please?

MOBYN: Are you seriously saying that for the sake of your bank balance Slim should stay his old, unenlightened self?

SLAYNE: Yes.

MOBYN: Just plundering and destroying without a social conscience?

SLAYNE: Yep

MOBYN: With no Marxist perspective on the capitalist nature of his adopted trade?

SLAYNE: You got it cowboy.

MOBYN: That he has no perceptions of culture in his immediate environment?

SLAYNE: If you mean the beauty of floating corpses and bloody tomahawks, then yes.

MOBYN: Good morning. I will not detain you any longer. A serious Publisher will back me and I'll be giving readings to Writers' circles and being interviewed by Mariella Frostrup.

SLAYNE: Hold on – just a minute. There must be a compromise. What About *Slim Saves the Prof* or.. or... *Gunfight in the OK Lecture Hall?*

SELF-PUBLISHERS AND SELF-PROMOTERS

MOBYN: (*leaving and slamming the door*) Good bye Mr Slayne

SLAYNE: *Dual in the School… or… Clever in the Saddle?*

*

Writers, when they assemble for conferences, discussions and support sessions, invariably talk about 'rewrites' and the associated trials and terrors. This stems from several sources of perceived unsuitability. It may be that the publisher wants the book changed so that it meets the demands of the current market more closely; it may be that the style and voice are not what that writer's faithful readership wants. Most autobiographies of writers, or documentary profiles of writers' lives, tend to dwell on this: the painful process of shaping up a typescript to meet the demands of (a) their agent, (b) the publisher (c) the reader. My own experience of this includes a short story I had once written. Its word count was 8,000 words, and the editor of an anthology would publish it – if I could reduce it to 2,500 words. I managed to do it, but I can't explain how. I recall sitting up late, typescript before me, and the red pen out, reducing, rephrasing, cutting out chunks of description, and so on.

The point was? Well, I learned that I was a relentless waffler. I remember wondering how on earth I could have essentially the same story, 6,000 words cut out? It made me look at everything in the notebooks – the rejected stories and poems – looking for padding. It was true, I liked the look of my own writing style, and it had been fatal. I was reminded of some of the best advice I ever had on writing poetry- 'the more words, the more lies.'

Of course, there are writers who take to the craft of storytelling like a duck to water. There's the author of *King Solomon's Mines*, for instance. What is unique in Rider Haggard's achievement in his major works is the inclusion of the kind of man who would have been a rowing and rugger blue at Cambridge, rather than the intellectual taking tea and scones and discussing Greek grammar, and he seemed to know instinctively that there was an audience for that kind of hero. That middle ground location of his storyteller's gifts, matched with his instinctive talents as a writer made a winning combination. But surprisingly, it was something rather more romantic that inspired him to write. In an article for *The Idler* magazine, he wrote:

> 'About this time the face of a girl whom I saw in a church at Norwood Gave me the idea of writing a novel. The face was so perfectly beautiful, And at the same time so refined, that I felt I could fit a story to it Which would be worthy of a heroine similarly endowed. When next I saw Mr Trubner I consulted him on the subject. "You can write –it is certain that you can write. Yes do it..." '

Rider Haggard reflects that how he did it he knew not, but he aimed at producing a woman 'perfect in mind and body.' This was his first book, *Dawn*, very rarely discussed now, but his account of how it came to exist says a great deal about his rather bluff, forthright and uncomplicated approach to narrative. His faith as a writer was in producing prose, as Orwell would have it, 'clear as a window-pane.'

Then, although the coast may seem clear for success after success, even the established writer finds he may be rebuffed –

often, for carrying on writing the same thing in the same way. In 1821, the essayist and political writer, William Hazlitt, was comfortably situated as a leading light in the London periodical world. Despite being deeply smitten by the attractions of his landlady's daughter, Sarah Walker, he found time to write, always producing his essays in a series called table Talk. But in October, James Hessey, who ran one of the magazines Hazlitt wrote for, dropped in to have a chat, and confirmed that Hazlitt's recent work was not wanted. As one of Hazlitt's biographers has explained, quoting Hessey, the writer was 'so annoyed and cramped in his mind by the fear of alteration or objection and perhaps rejection altogether that he could not write freely as he was accustomed to do.' Still, there was a bonus. His unrequited love for Sarah led to the writing of some of his best work, in his book, *Liber Amoris*.

This inevitably leads to the conclusion that one spin-off from failure may well be that one dead-end leads to a highway heading for somewhere else. Hence the advice often given to writers – never throw anything away. That is all very well, but others may throw your manuscript away and then failure stares you in the face.

6

THE PLAY'S THE THING

Playwrights have suffered horrendous reviews, rebuffs and criticisms. Even Will Shakespeare was not above this censure. His best mate, Ben Jonson, wrote in his notebooks that he 'Shakespeare never blotted out line' and lamented the fact that he had never edited his work. He thought him too prolific, and of course, there was a spot of jealousy there.

It is a tempting thought- after all, plays are short. See them on a bookshelf, in smart print in a slim volume, and you might think, *I could do that. I could knock that up in two hours I reckon*. Such is the vanity and over-confidence of the writing breed. Hence their fall is long and hard and the lessons learned are at a price.

Of course, the point about writing plays is that the author tends to be there, to see rehearsals, watch the work grow and change, and then he or she sits among the public on opening night and prays that all will be well. But rejection, if it happens then, will be brutal and short. Literary history is packed with poor souls who have nightmares in which phrases such as ' Stop this awful piss' and 'Shoot the author' run around a loop in the brain. I often think of all the failed, reviled and abused playwrights in history who have not been able to revel in taking a bow and receiving applause – simply because they wrote a bad play. Anyone can do that. But the pit is not well known for the quality of mercy.

One outstanding example in British theatre was Noel Coward's 1927 fiasco as his play, *Sirocco*, failed. Coward had at first sent the script to Ivor Novello, and he saw that is was very poor, refusing the part of the leading man (and villain). But Coward had charm and persistence, and he wined and dined Ivor until the great Welsh man of the theatre gave in and agreed to do it. But Ivor, though handsome, was not capable of playing a shady Lothario, and on the opening night, the less well-mannered members of the audience hissed and booed.

When the unstoppable and courageous Noel Coward decided to face the pit at the curtain-call, and walk with the leading lady towards the crowd to take a bow, someone called out, 'Hide behind your mother would you?' The audience were more than restless: they were out to create a farce. *The Times* reported on the members of the stalls: ' They were scarcely less well-disposed towards the other warriors who had played their parts in the battle… but when Mr Coward appeared, the mood of the house angrily changed. Even then the curtain was not allowed to remain down. Until Miss Doble … was thrust forward to make a speech, the hubbub continued. A more uncomfortable conclusion to an evening may we never experience.'

Coward was not the only writer whose work sometimes failed on the stage. The great novelist, Henry James, wrote a one-act comedy called *Summercroft* for Ellen Terry, but that never happened and James converted it into a short story, and then later into a very different play. As for Coward: his later career leaves no doubt that he could write original and hugely successful plays, songs and almost every other kind of theatrical entertainment. I guess he never had nightmares about that night in 1927 when the mob took over.

The Abbey Theatre Riot

There are not many times in the history of drama and literature that a work of art causes riots in the streets and in public buildings, but one of those times, and it was a very stirring and worrying event, was in Dublin, and at the very heart of what we now think of as the Irish Literary Renaissance. It had the poet Yeats shouting at the audience and playwright John Synge suffering all kinds of soul-searching stress and unease as his masterpiece seemed to split society apart.

Literature in Ireland has always had that tendency to be political and therefore to be misunderstood; in a country which has had so many invaders, so many internal divisions and such extreme struggles over ideas as well as over land and property, it comes as no surprise to learn that its writers can very easily be defined as somehow falling short of the mark. But in the case of John Synge and his play, The Playboy of the Western World, on the surface it seems bizarre that there should have been such hatred and resentment in the public. It is a play in which a son murders a father, or thinks he has, and there is a certain depiction of the West of Ireland peasantry that can be read as highly critical. Yet at the basis of Synge's art there is his fascination with folklore, rural communities and with the language and dialect of parts of the world which have not seen much social change.

To make matters worse, the trouble happened at the Abbey Theatre in Marlborough Street, Dublin. As I write this in 2017, The Playboy of the Western World has been performed at that very theatre; there were no riots and no dissent. But the Ireland of 1907 was a very different place, with many more uncertainties, sensitivities and doubts about itself and its direction.

John Synge was born in Rathfarnham in 1871. He studies at Trinity College and also at the Royal Irish Academy of Music. For three years after 1899 he lived with the Aran Islanders and developed a strong interest in the history, language and culture of the West of Ireland. This experience was 'material' for his plays and also for his book on the Aran Islands. He became friendly with W B Yeats, who helped and encouraged him, and he was then involved in the founding of the Abbey Theatre. He was never really well, suffering from Hodgkin's Disease, and he was to die just two years after the riots in response to his Playboy story.

The theatre was in the habit of keeping new productions under covers, but various people looked at the script, and saw Synge at work in rehearsals, and there was discussion about the need to do some cuts. Willie Fay wanted some of the more cruel details taken out, and Synge did cut some lines, but not to the satisfaction of Lady Gregory, who wrote in her memoirs that ' I told Synge that the cuts were not enough… I took out many phrases… which, ever since that first production, have not been spoken on our stage.'

Synge agreed to cut some 'bad language' but there was one key passage that stayed in, and it was certain to provoke anger; this was: 'It's Pegeen I'm seeking only, and what I'd care if you brought me a drift of chosen females, standing in their shifts itself, maybe, from this place to the eastern world?' But Synge continued to defend his art on the grounds that his language was only what he had heard spoken. He said he had heard expressions word for word. And that 'the central incident of the Playboy was suggested by an actual occurrence in the west.'

Although there were rumours of possible complaints and some aggressive reactions, there was no overt fear of any trouble on the horizon; an audience primarily made up of nationalists of various shades would be expected to be sympathetic in some ways. But that was a gross miscalculation. The opening night came along, and at first the crowd were quiet, but then the speech about the 'shifts' caused a stir. The audience started hissing and booing. One man wrote after the first performance that Synge was the 'evil genius' of the Abbey theatre. People tried to comfort the sick and stressed playwright with words such as ' ...it's better to have the row we had last night than to have your play fizzling out in half-hearted applause.' But there was far worse to come.

With Lady Gregory, who was a joint founder of the Abbey in 1904, Synge decided to call in the police for the second performance; after all the Irish Times had made it clear that the play was scandalous, saying, 'what in other respects was a brilliant success' had finally 'an inglorious conclusion.' What really counted though, in terms of whipping up nationalist fervour and old-fashioned morality was the opinion of The Freeman's Journal as it supported the moderate nationalist Irish Party under

John Redmond, and unfortunately the verdict there was that the play was 'an unmitigated, protracted libel upon Irish peasant men, and worse, upon Irish peasant girlhood.. The blood boils with indignation as one recalls the incidents, expressions, ideas, of his squalid, offensive production, incongruously styled a comedy…'

On the next performance, there were police present by the vestibule door. William Fay, who played the lead role, said that the audience had become 'a veritable mob of howling devils.' The row became a real riot and the crowd were about to storm the stage itself when there was a feat of remarkable fortitude buy a call-boy, who grabbed a huge axe and stood before them, saying that he swore by all the saints in the calendar that eh would chop the head off the first lad who came over the footlights.'

Fay begged the protesters to go, and promised that they would have their money back; but the crowd yelled, 'Kill the author!' As performances went on regardless, things escalated. The audience stamped their feet and fights broke out. Finally, after the worst responses, there were five hundred police called out on duty and a reporter said they were 'as think as blackberries in September.'

On the Tuesday performance, the great poet, W B Yeats arrived and tried to act to save the situation, but when he addressed the restless audience that night, he said that the people making the row were philistines, that 'they had no books in their houses' and that they were 'commonplace and ignorant people.' That did not really improve things. He shouted at the audience 'We have put this play before you to be heard and to be judged..

The country that condescends either to bully or to permit itself to be bullied soon ceases to have any fine qualities...'

On Wednesday night there was a fist fight. There were fifty police officers in the aisles, but still there was violence and then later, in the streets, there was a rowdy procession. Matters had to lead to the magistrate's court, and Yeats was there to testify against the offenders, and they were fined ten shillings each. But things settled down by the Friday performance and there was only one arrest then.

As David Greene wrote in his biography of John Synge, ' The most tumultuous event in Dublin theatrical history was over, though the debate over the man who had slain his da was to rage for weeks to come and the riots were to be repeated years later in places as remote from Dublin as New York and Montreal.'

The first inkling of trouble was when Lady Gregory sent a simple telegram to the author with the message: ' Play broke up in disorder at the word shift.' As has been pointed out by various writers, if only Synge had used another word, things might not have got out of hand. But the whole experience did nothing to help his already delicate state of health and he took to his bed with a severe 'flu infection for weeks afterwards.

Writers have recorded similar problems with single words. Often in a poetry reading, it is not the wrong word but the obscure word that causes the problem. This is doubly troublesome with dialect of course. I once staged a poetry reading for my students, and there was an open mic session. I had a Glaswegian student who was keen to read, but all the class were aware that his speech had to be deciphered by we poor southerners. Yet how could I refuse to give him his three minutes? The result may be imagined. It had the same effect that Rabbie Burns must have had with his *wee sleeket cowerin beasties* when he did his first gig in Edinburgh. After the performance, there were polite claps but lots of mutterings, and the phrase *What was that all about?* Dominated the discussion later.

In spite of knowing about such nasty refusals to accept the writer's craft by his audience, I still thought that the thing to do was write for the stage. This was my first effort, destined to be liked but rejected. Responses were mixed: *We felt that it lacked contemporary bite…* or *suitable for a sixth-form jolly…*

*

Plan B for me, in the trajectory of my failures with the pen, was to write for the screen but I did nothing more than plan out an epic drama that was to mix Genghis Khan with a factory worker from Bradford. Then I saw the light: what people wanted was poetic drama. I sat up all night working hard on what was essentially a spoof of *The Waste Land*. I thought it was wonderful. I was wrong; it went into the waste paper basket of course. What I did do, though, which was some kind of success, was start to write for the poetry magazine, *Agenda*.

I was stunned to find that the editors did not reply with rejection slips, and that once again, I had stumbled upon a writer/poet/editor in Peter Dale, who offered advice on improving the poems I sent for consideration. As well as lyric poetry, Peter Dale had established a reputation as a writer of verse drama. I saw then that yes, it could be done. The result was my attempt at a long verse drama about Lord Tennyson, but unfortunately it read like Betjeman marred by McGonagall, and so it was committed to oblivion.

Success of a kind had arrived: I contributed to *Agenda* for almost twenty years and was a published poet in a celebrated London-based magazine. Be still, my beating heart!

But I came to see that success was avoiding me because I was trying too hard. Making the meaning clear, over-explaining, was cramping the style. I became aware of the pitfalls of this habit when I encountered the poems of Edward Edwin Foot, who was a customs officer, but in his spare time he took to writing verse. The gentleman was of such a particular, officious state of mind that he felt his poetic references needed to be explained. Naturally, this habit tended to put off would-be publishers. For instance, in one poem he has a line, ' The captain scans the ruffled zone' and then feels he has to have a foot-note to explain that this is 'to signify the horizon.' In short, Mr Foot had no poetic feet, or at least, he failed in his attempts to scan them. He, as it were, put a Foot wrong…

In the social history of the theatre, overdoing it was the surest way to be rejected. This is plain to see in the dramatic efforts of literary men, those who were bookish and so quite capable of writing essays or criticism, but when they tried to write for the theatre, they failed. One such case is that of Samuel Taylor Coleridge, a perfectly wonderful poet and a rare variety of thinker, but when he tried his hand at writing for the stage, the result was tragic. In 1797 his play, *Osorio*, was rejected by the great dramatist, Richard Brinsley Sheridan. But in 1813, it was, amazingly for Coleridge, accepted for production by the new management at Drury Lane.

However, the actors and professionals took hold of the play and cut, trimmed and reshaped it, giving it a new title of *Remorse: A Tragedy in Five Acts*, and it did very well, earning Coleridge plenty of money, and doing the rounds in the provinces as well.

Not so fortunate in his efforts to become a playwright was Samuel Johnson. The story of his leaving Lichfield, along with his friend, David Garrick, both to seek their fortunes in London, would lead one to believe that Sam could not fail to succeed if he tried his hand at writing a play. Indeed he did write one – called *Irene* – and the result was a warning to all literary men who feel that there is easy money to be made by writing for the stage.

Irene opened at Drury Lane on February 6, 1749. Johnson had written in twelve years before this, in his late twenties, and by the time Garrick took it and pushed it, which he could do as he was the manager of the theatre, the world had changed, and the theatre also. Audiences at that time made their opinions known in a forthright and robust way, and Johnson's play stirred the pit to action. After a lengthy argument, Garrick had made some changes to make the play more in line with current fashion, but made one radical change in having Irene, who has to die by strangling, actually killed on stage before the audience, rather than off stage, behind.

Johnson, not known for his elegance of dress and sense of fashion, had clearly talked himself into thinking that this was the beginning of a splendid career as a dramatist, and accordingly he wore dandyism attire even having a scarlet waist-coat and a hat trimmed with gold. The audience were loud, and then more than loud when the actress playing Irene came on stage and events showed that she was destined to 'die' before their eyes. Such was the power of the pit that Garrick gave in and had the woman taken out of view to be strangled.

The 'Great Cham' of literature, in spite of this farcical situation, found that his one play had a run of nine nights and had brought a sum of £195 at the door. On top of that, it was printed and made £100 profit. In 1749 this was a huge sum. In the overall context of Johnson's work, the play is usually seen as his notable failure, but arguably, it was a 'nice little earner' for him. Generally, readers never think of Johnson as a young man; the well-known pictures of him all depict the overweight, unhealthy older man he became. But when he set off for London from Lichfield, with his friend David, he was young, ambitious and certainly not lacking in self-belief. He knew that he could earn his living by his pen, but he soon learned that the theatre was not his real *metier*.

Theatre in the Blood: Dodie Smith

In the history of theatre, there are a myriad tales of flops- everything from short runs such as *Irene*, down to plays that were destined never to go beyond rehearsal. Yet one aspect of the history of play-writing stands out: if the writer has acting, fooling and playing around in them from childhood, they stand a fighting chance of success. Dodie Smith, well known for her novel, *The One Hundred and One Dalmatians,* was such a writer. Not only did she have a whole bunch of thespian aunts and uncles in her childhood in Manchester: she wrote a journal, which included snatches of fiction, from a very early age. Consequently, when she went into acting, the thought of writing plays was as natural to her as writing about everything else.

When her family moved to London, after her mother's second marriage, Dodie went to St Paul's school, where the music master was Gustav Holst, and she flowered in the English classes, beginning her writing in print with work for the school magazine. Then in 1914 she took the entrance exam for RADA. She was given a place, but she was soon to be orphaned, as her mother died (her father had died at only thirty, back in Manchester).

Remarkably, she began with success: it was also the time when she tried to make it as a writer, producing a screenplay for a silent movie, writing with the name of Charles Henry Percy, and it was bought for £3.10s. But there was a dip. As her biographer, Valerie Grove wrote: it 'the first and last money she was to earn from writing for sixteen years.'

She turned to the stage, and met other similar girls at the Three Arts Club. Her life became that of the jobbing actress, living in bed-sits and taking small parts. Then in 1922 she was given a job in a bookshop, then took her last acting role, and wrote in her diary: 'I was on my own at last, and determined to earn money by writing.' This would have to happen while she was earning money as a shop-girl.

She produced a play called *Pirate Ships,* which appears to have been lost to posterity; then came *Autumn Crocus*, sent to an agent, and Geoffrey Whitworth responded with: ' This is a difficult play. The tale is a sour one. But it is extremely well written and the characters are admirably drawn.' What happened next was that a reader for the London Play Company liked the script, and it was also read by Nigel Playfair. Things were definitely promising, and the turning point came when Basil Dean became aware of it. He had directed Dodie Smith some years before in a play in Manchester, so he knew the name. She sold the play: success at last, after a very long gap in which she had acted on the fringe, worked long hours in a shop, and felt the rejection of her first effort.

Dodie went on to write several successful plays and novels, including *Dear Octopus* in 1938 and of course, *The One Hundred and One Dalmatians* in 1956. Her story gives us the heartening message that a long gestation period pays off: she had a decade or more with no writing being presented to publishers. But when the moment came for the first real play, the waiting time had been a period of absorption and understanding of her subject-matter.

7

CASE STUDIES IN REJECTION AND SUCCESS

This is the point in my account of failure that the concept of success should be introduced. Surely, failure may only be understood in terms relative to success. What, then, is success? The word runs away as soon as you try to define it.

It ought to be something defined in the individual's own terms. The media today tend to define it as being a celebrity, but that is simply a cliché. The easiest option, in trying to understand a word, is to go for the plain example- so if you are always on TV then you must be a success. Therein lies the powerful deception which works by indoctrination, and aspiring writers love the carrot of fame and popularity. A poem published in a local paper may be used to define success just as much as a poetry collection winning a major literary prize for its author. This is all very well, but means nothing in the cut and thrust world of creative writing and publishing. Great, humming, cackling herds of authors at conferences, book launches, bookish celebrations and general literati do's reflect friendship, of course, but they also contain within them extremes of rancour, envy, constant jealousy and competitiveness. The author's eyes are always on sales, and in between e-mails, blogs and tweets, the struggling author has regular visits to the Amazon site to check on sales and reviews.

Success is?

Success, in the modern age, may have the personal perspective, but it also has the nature of being so desirable that writers may develop their elbowing-out muscles to stay ahead in their genre. There are writers who work like slaves to push, mention, plug, sell and talk about their new book, aware that behind them are a thousand other writers wanting their slot in the publisher's schedule.

This is a world of success measured as media presence, status as a blogger, the writer's image as a celebrity, the frequency and attitude of reviewers and so on. Therefore failure is in inverse proportion to that: you sink, and you sink very low. Not being noticed is to be rejected. If a slippage is noted, then for the sake of Saint Gilbert, change your brand, your face, your level of toadying, and ratchet up your bare-faced cheek.

All this leads to such fear of failure that the degree of desperation to achieve success become snot merely intense but not a little bonkers. I know one unpublished novelist at a conference who shoved her typescript under the look door when she knew that an agent was inside, doing her business. At a major conference in Denver once, I stepped out of a lift, along with ten other writers, to be greeted by a young lady who held out a fistful of business cards and told us that she was Lindy, '... and this is my first novel.'

In the twenty-first century we are used to seeing things with an acceptance of the complexity in their nature and their functions. In the sometimes esoteric microcosm of the creative writing course, with its seminars and workshops, there is often a disservice done to aspiring writers- the tendency never to criticise work read or read aloud. As a tutor in that area of work, I have experienced thousands of such situations, in which something is read aloud to the group and it becomes clear that there is a general feeling that it has been flat, perhaps rather boring, or maybe too pretentious. But what happens? There are mumblings of general admiration and everything said refers to the positive. People search for complimentary things to say, avoiding any condemnation or critical demolition.

Digging a little deeper in this, it has to be said that writing itself is non-commercial anyway; creative users of language are primarily enjoying a dialogue with the self. All literature is, in some sense, autobiographical. At heart, language at its most imaginative, when it is most split from the shared reality of the reader and writer, is utterly separate from any marketplace. In a sense, we writers are all like Coleridge's Ancient Mariner: we stoppeth one of three' with our long tale and try the reader's/listener's patience. It's ten to one on the poor victim has no interests in an albatross shot at sea. He maybe would just prefer going to get some fish and chips.

One of the most profound shocks that beginning writers experience in their first creative writing workshop is that there is such a concept as writing for some kind of identified or specified reader- writing for someone else, as it were. Research by Greg

Light in 1999 offers an explanation of the common stages of development we (most of us) have in the ways in which we change and progress as writers. He posits a number of stages in which we write with a reader awareness, and he notes that we tend to engage in 'releasing' and 'documenting' in our first phases. In those early stages, we are primarily engaged in trying to understand out lives, and the formative influences which have taken us to the point at which we start to write.

With that in mind, common sense tells us that when we move to later stages (which Light calls *narrating* and *critiquing*) we absorb knowledge of a perceived reader. Hence, in the world of publishing now, editors, publishers and agents will expect writers to be aware of their defined readership.

Yet all this is very recent. Over the course of the last century, rejection and failure have been 'the school of life' as far as most writers are concerned. Many successful writers recall their false starts very well. Katie Fforde, trying to write for Mills and Boon, was told she 'lacked sparkle.' Her publishing success since that proves that she learned how to shine in such a way that she knows her readership very well now.

The Slips keep Coming

Sylvia Plath once wrote, ' I love my rejection slips. They show me I try.' That is a very rare attitude among the writing fraternity. More typical is the little domestic tragedy George Orwell gives us in what is perhaps the novel which deals more thoroughly with literary failure than any other work. The writer in question is poet Gordon Comstock, author of one slim volume of verse with the title of *Mice*; the book is *Keep the Aspidistra Flying* (1936). Very little in the entire and miserable situation of the rejected author is omitted. Comstock lives alone, living in a bed-sit and working for a pittance in a bookshop. He has refused to live a life dominated by money and materialism, and so he becomes the modern exponent of the starving writer in the garret template. Chatterton, arguably the first such scribbler, took his own life at just seventeen – a real tragedy. Comstock, however, endures and lives stoically, eventually falling in love and rising above his ideals.

In his analysis of Comstock, Orwell brilliantly depicts the struggling writer, persisting in producing poems and sending them to editors, knowing that they will be returned, and that the arrival of a bulky envelope rather than a slim one, will damage his self-esteem yet again. We have Comstock waiting for the post, nervously expecting the decision of the editor of the usually highbrow magazine he has chosen. However, he does know one editor, the wealthy young editor of the journal *Antichrist*, Ravelston. Comstock's poems are occasionally printed by Ravelston, but everywhere else he fails, in spite of the fact that Mice had been reviewed by the *Times Literary Supplement* and their comment had been that the work showed 'exceptional promise.'

Orwell's novel is surely the definitive study of the failed writer. His insistence on living his life of dismal anonymity leads to the depths of ignominy, such as his arrival at a party supposed to be given by a literary critic; Comstock has worn his one decent outfit of clothes, and is looking forward to free food and drinks. Then the party, he finds, has been cancelled and everyone else has been told. Comstock, a nobody, has not even been deemed important enough to be told that the party is off. His poems have been rejected by *The Primrose Quarterly*, the party is cancelled, and later, Mice is in the bargain box, 'reduced to threepence.'

As authorship became a viable career for those people who had risen to the ranks of the literate, thanks to the Education Act of 1870 and the emergence of elementary education, books and periodicals multiplied. There was a need for writers to fill the pages of the multiplying publications of the press, both popular and highbrow. Writers gradually learned how to understand the intricacies involved in writing for a genre, and how to respond to the needs of an identified readership.

This new version of the professional author made demands: the poor slave of the typewriter had to write the story but also give a great deal of thought to everything commercial, such as the title. The decision in that respect was vital. William Golding, for instance, a man with office work in his c.v., may well have called his masterpiece *Lord of the Files.* Jane Lovering, the novelist, had a sarcastic response from one publisher, referring to '*The White Crystal*, if that's what it is called....' Nagging doubts were thus cast in Jane's mind, and a problem with a title can spread like a virus to every aspect of a work in progress.

In the early twentieth century we have the case of an author who found success late, and whose career illustrates the fundamental dichotomy between 'literature' and 'writing.' His career is in line with Micky Spillane's comment that there are writers and there are authors.. the difference is that writers get paid. I refer to Raymond Chandler, creator of Philip Marlowe and those crime classics, *Farewell, My Lovely* and *The Big Sleep*. Chandler was over fifty when he found real success as a popular novelist, although he had published poetry in his twenties. He defines literary failure not in general terms, but in that fascinating area of interest to all creative writing aspirants: finding what one writes best.

Working in London, fresh from having a classical education at Dulwich College, he wrote poems for *Chambers' Journal*, the first one in print by 1906. The poems are neo-romantic and verbose, and Chandler himself told an interviewer that he was 'fortunate in not possessing a copy.' His biographer, Frank MacShane, told his readers that they were less fortunate and printed one, "The Unknown Love" in his book on Chandler. To be fair, Chandler did write other things for several journals, but as MacShane comments, 'Chandler understood the need for a literary vision, but he did not have one himself.' Chandler himself was always denigrating himself, applying the deadpan phrases he gave to his character Marlowe, and at one time he said that he could become a 'second-rate anything.'

But then, the 'failure' discovered the fiction magazine, *Black Mask*. This is a perfect example of the version of literary failure which is merely a setback, a temporary lapse. He had gone through what most writers experience: literary influences, ranging from Keats in his poetry, to Saki in his first tentative short stories. Then he read Dashiell Hammett.

*

But there have always been intellectual creative types and eccentrics in the ranks of the writers of course, and not all of them have cared much about genre or readership. To many such characters, writing is a game as well as a profession. Take Fernando Pessoa for instance, the Portuguese poet. He had seventy-two different *noms de plumes* and was in the habit of writing savage reviews on the work of his alter egos. This is in complete contrast, of course, to the modern examples of writers who write positive and glowing reviews of their own book on Amazon.

Crazily, it is almost as of the poet in Pessoa wanted to experience failure, criticism and attacks on the quality of his work, as a way to keep on improving. Or maybe in negating the 'failed' other selves, he was reminding himself how successful the writer called *Fernando Pessoa* really was?

'Failures' Behind Bars

Such oddities sit uneasily beside the location or surely the most significant instance of rejection in the world of writing in the last century: soviet Russia. In that context, 'failure' meant an inability to be acceptable to the political regime, of course. yet many of the writers thrown in jail or sent into oblivion have come out as success stories in the end. The great poet and translator, Joseph Brodsky, for instance, was sent to the wilds of Archangel for the offence of 'social parasitism' and so he had been rejected as a writer, but in his failure there was still the seed of success.

There is nothing quite like a prison sentence in a gulag to inform you, as a writer, that the state considers you to be a failure.

Research has shown that, by 1920, when the Revolution and the ensuing civil war had raged across the continent, two prison systems were in place in the new Soviet Union. The usual, established criminal prison establishment was organised by the Commissariat of Justice, with an element of corrective labour; in contrast, the Cheka , later the OGPU and KGB, controlled what were at first known as special camps. The import fact about the latter is that they were outside the normal criminal justice system. Their administration was unknown and was closed t all but authorised persons, such as the official visit to Solovetsky by the writer Maxim Gorky in 1929. This camp system, which became the Gulag from the words *Glavnoe upravlenie lagerei*, equated to one of the most terribly resonant acronyms in Russian history. It was to last until Stalin's death in 1953.

At first, there was confusion and great disparity in the treatment of prisoners across the land; the prisoners of the Cheka were the intelligentsia and other deviants, and there was a period of overlap before Lenin's penal philosophy was consolidated. Therefore, in some prisons there was what seems on the surface to be an enlightened regime, as at the Moscow Butirka prison, where inmates had clean linen, books and health care; but in contrast, at Arkhangelsk, as Anne Applebaum relates, matters were extreme and brutal: ' Brodsky did not have a good time.

Stalin's writers and poets were always in a precarious position: did they write in praise of the tractor, or was the current tractor about to be scrapped, and so therefore did one write in praise of the new tractor? After all, poets, as much as factory workers, were living under the threatening shadow of premature obsolescence. The latest fashionable ode could be erased as rapidly as the latest coal lorry.

Let's be honest, literary failure doesn't get as extreme as a situation in which the author is made a non-person. Yet, paradoxically, a failed writer who is locked up because he or she is writing unacceptable material may actually find that prison energises their creativity. This was suggested by the Chilean poet, Pablo Neruda, writing about Nazim Hikmet, the Turkish writer who was imprisoned in the 1930s. Neruda wrote, ' Nazim's lyrical work reached its greatest there. Hi voice became the voice of the world; William Armstrong, writing about Hikmet, adds, 'Whatever harm it did to his physical and mental health, prison was the making of Hikmet's poetry.'

Back in the terrifying days of the Regency in Britain, when the authorities were shivering with fear that a revolution might happened here, copying that in France, and when debt also led to jail, writers and artists were always liable to fail by being taken out of circulation. This was the lot of many a writer, and perhaps the best example is that of William Combe – a name not known today, but in his time he was an extraordinary hack, and played a part in the history of *The Times* newspaper.

Combe is a figure of paradox and contradiction, and this was made more extreme by his unknown and uncertain years, and also by his sheer breadth of interests and publications. When he married Maria Foster, wife of a former school friend, in 1776, he was described in the press as ' A gentleman who is universally known, from having distinguished himself in this, and other countries, in various shapes and characters.' He was at Eton College, and later after the death of his father he had a guardian called William Alexander, after whose death in 1762, Combe inherited considerable wealth. There was something of the dreamer and the actor in him: he fancied himself as a gentleman among the dandies and rakes, and signed himself 'Esquire.' Yet he was in some ways entirely typical of the young men of his generation; like Rowlandson he travelled in France, but was apparently penniless by 1770. His activities in the 1770s are a mystery: he may have been a soldier, and that never worked out, just as the earlier intention of having a legal career never worked out either.

What he did do well was make friendships and enter into a range of employment, developing himself as a jack of all trades. One close friend was the writer Laurence Sterne, author of *Tristram Shandy*; but by 1773 he had made his first venture into the lower reaches of the literary world, when he was given the chance of editing a book by Thomas Falkner called *A Description of Patagonia*. That was a common way into hack writing, just as Dr Johnson had done when he translated a work on Abyssinia (as it was then). After that there was no stopping him, and with remarkable energy he wrote a play, *The Flattering Milliner*, which was staged in Bristol; what he did latch on to was the public's affection for parody. He wrote a volume of letters purporting to be written by Sterne to others, called Letters to his Friends on Various occasions. Combe the master of pastiche and copyist style was born.

In the 1770s he was well known – despite the fact that his early books were anonymous it was commonly known that he was the author. He was very much a journalist with an eye to topicality. In 1771 Henry Mackenzie published *The Man of Feeling* and it was a great success: it was no more that sketches of 'the new man' – one of refined sensibility and social grace. It had such an impact that it influenced various other writers including Charles Lamb. Richard Sheridan spoofed the whole notion in 1777 with his play, *The School for Scandal*. For Combe, it was there to be exploited, and he wrote The Philosopher in Bristol (1775). It explains much about Combe that this was self-published: he was desperate to strike while the iron was hot, even though it meant a rash experiment financially.

The core of survival in the Regency years for any number of people in all walks of life was the desperate search for financial security, with a universal search for patronage and for other ways of surviving in the arts by any possible means. Combe was entirely typical in this. It was an age when, for instance, large numbers of people managed to live in sinecures and pensions, doing very little. As a publication of 1819 called *The Extraordinary Red Book* shows, there were such posts as clerk to the dockyards, with pay of £100 per annum, along with thousands of pensioners such as Lady Collingwood who received £1,000 per annum and her two daughters each received £500 simply for being her companions. Crowds waited in levee for favours of the rich, scribes and hacks wrote letters begging for patronage, and a lower rank of hacks hung around the booksellers of St Paul's trying to live on pence for writing paragraphs, obituaries and reviews. Combe was one who tried patronage and when it failed, he ridiculed the rich instead. The Regent (George, later George IV) himself loved portraiture and if, like Thomas Lawrence, a painter could specialise in doing flattering portraits, then patronage might be more possible. But for the Combes of the world, the printers and booksellers had the power, and with Combe in mind, it is worth noting that the writers generally did rather better than the painters in terms of the Regent's attention. As Donald Low put it: ' … It made a difference to the social and intellectual climate that the Regent was as ready to talk with poets as with statesmen, and to confer a baronetcy on Walter Scott; in this way writers were made to feel that they counted for something in society.'

In fact cash- the lack of it - became the formative influence on his life. Perhaps the stem of this was his debts related to the expense of keeping his wife in an asylum run by Stephen Casey at Plaistow in Essex. From the early 1780s he turned his attention to the easiest route to reputation in literature: he wrote satires. On e of his targets was Simon Luttrell, Baron Irnham and later Earl of Carhampton. In 1744 he bought his country seat, Four Oaks, in Warwickshire, and by 1754 he was M P for Michael in Cornwall. Combe and others saw him as an excellent satirical target, and one ballad has him as a candidate for the title of King of Hell: 'But as he spoke there issued from the crowd/ Irnham the base, the cruel and the proud/ and eager cried, "I boast superior claim/ To Hell's dark throne and Irnham is my name.'

His career up to meeting and working with artist Thomas Rowlandson was mixed, uncertain and risky; but one thing he did do which turned out to be successful was work with the new *Times* newspaper. When the writer and diarist Henry Crabb Robinson, wrote his memoirs near the end of his long life (he died in 1867) he had known virtually everyone of any note in the Romantic literature and culture of the time, and he had known Combe earlier in his life when Robinson was foreign editor and Combe was a regular contributor to what was then the *Daily Universal Register* but which would become *The Times*. Robinson gives us this impression of Combe:

> *'I understand that he was a man of fortune when young, and travelled in Europe and even made a journey with Sterne; that he ran through his fortune, and took to literature, when house and land were gone and spent, and when his high connections ceased to be of service... I used to enjoy the anecdotes he told after dinner, until one day, when he had been very communicative, and I had sucked in all he related with a greedy ear, Fraser said, laughing to Walter, "Robinson, you see is quite a flat... he believes all that old Combe says."'*

Robinson was embarrassed that he had been too credulous, but the tale tells us a lot about Combe when he was older:

REJECTED

he clearly had been minor celebrity in his time, and was still a good talker, but there was the 'imitator' of old – that man who had written so much in imitation of others, for laughs and for satire, was later perhaps out of control in that respect and exaggerated everything for the sake of a good story.

Combe was sixty-six when he began his four years in prison; this was in 1808 and in that year, Ackermann needed a writer to handle the text for the last volume of the series, The Microcosm of London, to work with Rowlanfdson and his drawings, and Combe stepped in. Combe's biographer points out that the vast output that followed, writing that kept him busy behind bars and out on what we would today call licence, was not all hackwork. He writes:

> 'The compilation of seven hundred pages on Westminster Abbey... required a diligent search for information, and many volumes of antiquarian lore must have been brought to his quarters while he was performing this assignment.
> There was certainly a library in the Bench, yet Combe manages to cite learned authorities....'

He definitely had a scholarly ability, and he could cope with that as well as with real journeyman penny a line material. Between 1810 and 1822 he produced fourteen solid volumes of topography and contributed a massive amount of material to such publications as would give him column inches.

The lesson in this tale of woe? Stick at it- inside or outside the nick. There's an opening somewhere – and never throw any script away.

CASE STUDIES IN REJECTION AND SUCCESS

Charles Lamb Boos his own play

Charles Lamb, famous as the author of the classic book of prose humour, *The Essays of Elia*, and with his sister Mary, of Tales from Shakespeare, was a lover of the theatre. His works are packed with affectionate tributes to old actors, people whose careers flourished a short time and then, as Shakespeare wrote, 'had their hour upon the stage' and were 'heard no more.' Charles adored the stage and the whole world of the theatre so much that he tried his hand at writing his own pieces. He wrote a play called Mr H which was premiered on 10 December, 1806.

The great essayist witnessed a notable failure, but he took it on the chin. He had plenty of friends there on the night to cheer and to make the right noises, but, as he wrote in a letter to his friend William Wordsworth, 'The quantity of friends we had in the house, my brother and I being in the public offices… was astonishing, but they yielded at length to a few hisses.. A hundred hisses- damn the word, I write it like kisses – how different – a hundred hisses outweigh a thousand claps.. Well, 'tis withdrawn and there's an end.'

The evening began well, because the prologue was well liked. William Hazlitt, who was there, later wrote his response:

> ' How often did I conjure up in recollection the full diapason of applause at
> The end of the prologue, and hear my ingenious friend in the front row of
> The pit roar with laughter at his own wit…To a public fed on the broad
> Dramatic fun of Colman… there was nothing satisfying in a farce the chief
> Humour of which turned upon a grotesque surname.'

Lamb's character was Hogsflesh, and he had tried to squeeze out plenty of fun from that, but to no avail. However, as Lamb's biographers have pointed out, the management still tended to advertise Mr H as a success. But The Theatrical Examiner published a summing-up of the sorry failure:

> Mr H thou art damned. Bright shone the morning on the play-bills
> That announced they appearance, and the streets were full with the buzz
> Of persons asking one another if they would go and see Mr H, and
> Answering that they would certainly, but before night the gaiety, not
> Of the author, but of his friends and the town, was eclipsed, for thou
> Wert damned! Hadst thou been anonymous, thou haply mightst have lived.

The author was not totally discouraged though. He told his sister that he planned to write another farce, with all that experience 'on his head.'

Sadly, Charles Lamb's other dramatic works have been consigned to oblivion too. When did you ever see an advert for John Woodvil, A tragedy, or The Pawnbroker's Daughter: A Farce? On the credit side, his essays and autobiographical pieces are always in print, and he is seen as a massive influence on many writers of his time.

There are so many varieties of failure of course. Here we must have a look at the handbooks and guides, written by successful writers, and aimed at the strugglers down in the land of screwed-up rejection slips and flat egos. These books, and the articles in popular writing magazines, often make it seem as though avoiding rejection is as simple as dodging sunshine in a British November. In reality, it's as easy as getting a Christmas sun-tan.

That is how it looks, from a distance, but in reality, even very successful authors usually have a tale to tell. Recently (August, 2013) a web site featuring an analysis of the percentage of unfinished reads asserted, surprisingly, that *Fifty Shades of Grey* and also J K Rowling's new novel (non-Potter) each had a low percentage. In other words, many readers said that they were bored and stopped reading long before the last page. There's a type of failure that most authors never know anything about.

Enemies of Promise

However, failure at the beginning of successful careers is a topic that shocks the aspiring writer, and many writers have such horrific stories to tell when they are interviewed or when they write their memoirs. Peter Carey, for instance, author of several highly-rated novels, told such a story of struggle and ill fortune when he was interviewed for *The Paris Review.* Carey had a keen response from a publisher in his native Australia; they said they loved the book and would publish it. When he met them, they went cool on him and made it clear that they had changed their minds. But, they informed Peter, a publisher from Britain was in Oz, scouting for talent, and that the manuscript had been given to him. A long time after that, after a long silence, Peter was in London, and went to the publisher to see what decision had been reached. He told his interviewer that the receptionist told him to wait a minute and then, ' She came back in fifteen minutes and gave me my manuscript, and said, thank you very much....'

Advice from writers, in thousands of creative writing guides, is so abundant that confusion may ensue; they all have comments to make about dealing with rejection. The most daunting part of this is that they usually itemize the types of rejection: those rebuffs effected by editors, publishers, agents, critique services, professional readers, and so on. In other words, notice of failure comes at the hapless scribe from all corners, and sometimes in rapid succession. What is the best advice?

Comforting thoughts for coping with any variety of rejection tend to be in these categories:

a) It is part of a learning curve. Be stoical
b) It is simply one person's opinion
c) They have bothered to write, so there is some talent there.
d) This is one way to learn that you are writing in the wrong genre
e) What do they know anyway?

Now, much of this can seem, to the tyro, like words of wisdom from Sherpa Tensing to a man with one leg down at base camp. However, something positive has to be taken from the thoughts of those who have struggled. Peter Carey did break into print. The trick is to evaluate the advice given. For instance, John Gardner, in his book, *On Becoming a Novelist*, gives some solid, professional guidance: ' Whereas after a certain number of rejections the writer is likely to give up on a story or a novel, the agency goes on….Agents usually know better than writers when to give up…' This is valuable – but of course, first you have to find an agent!

Gardner also adds that rejection by an agent means more than rejection by an editor. In other words, once in the business of having a completed manuscript, doing the rounds, rejection becomes far more significant. For those of us (most writers) who have no agent, our destiny is that place with the dreaded name – *the slush pile*.

Advice in the handbooks about rejection usually works by means of helping us either to avoid the slush pile or to feel fine if our work is in there, with at least a slim chance of being read within six months of receipt. The slush pile means the heap of unsolicited work which arrives daily at the publishers' offices, by post and not via an agent.

Beginner writers imagine this to be a stack of manila folders, each with a goodly wodge of papers inside it, going at least six feet above the desk of a junior editor. Who knows if this is or is not the truth? When I first tried my hand at writing fiction, I knew that the slush pile was the destination of my work, and I imagined the thing to be an unstable mountain of files, often slipping across the floor of some overheated den in a back office somewhere in the heart of London. I may have been right. All I asked for, even if rejected, was a coffee stain on page twenty, just to prove that it had actually been read. Then of course I came to realise that editors probably had a habit of placing a coffee cup on every page twenty of every script they had, just to offer some modicum of comfort to the poor Joe at the other end of the chain.

Encouragement must, however, be taken from the anecdotes we find in the recollections of seasoned, successful writers. Anne Mcallister, a prize-winning romance author, recalls a time when she had two books short-listed for the RITA award (annual awards of the Romance Writers of America) and her editor made a speech, saying to the assembled crowd that she wanted to publish anything by Anne. Not long after that, she rejected the next idea. But at least Anne won a RITA that year. The same author remembers a puzzling response which was a rejection and an acceptance, the editor writing that she liked the book 'the second time she read it.'

In the end, modern case studies reveal the simple principle of being persistent and try hard to make literary friends. Roger McGough, for instance, in an interview, explained that while he was a student at Hull, reading French and very much influenced by Arthur Rimbaud, he was lucky enough to have some feedback and encouragement from Philip Larkin, who was librarian there at the time. Mc Gough makes it clear, as several other successful writers have done, that writing is done for the love of the activity itself and that one has to believe in the rightness and quality of what one may produce. Of course, there is tremendous satisfaction in simply looking with pride at a finished piece of writing. Failure will never be an issue if a writer never goes beyond that.

Over the course of the last century, the sheer multiplicity of writers in print is astonishing; reputations come and go, and most failure is never known or acknowledged; the notorious 'second book blues' – known by very many novelists- testifies to that failure. A friend of mine was given a two-book contract after her first book was accepted by a large London publisher. The second book followed, and then, that was an end of her career. Such a pattern is very common. Failure tends to follow success: the greatest irony in the business, and the cause of much quiet Angst. The writer suffering that setback has to figure out a way to re-emerge. Today, the way to survive and the way to avoid 'the drop' is to be sure that you have a 'brand.' This telephone conversation probably happens on a daily basis now:

Agent: Ted, Ted… how are you buddy?

Writer: Fine… working on the new book… planning it out, you know.

Agent: Ah, I wanted to talk to you about that.

Writer: Is there a problem? It's a thriller, right?

Agent: Not exactly a problem Ted. That's a disturbing word. I don't want to disturb you. I know you're writing to your strengths. It's just that we're not sure that your Great War themes and settings are .. well, really what you're about.

Writer: Who's the 'we' then Peter?

Agent: We?

Writer: You just said 'we' with reference to me.

Agent: Oh, Jed the editor, yes… we, of course. It's just your brand, Ted. That's the issue. You need a new one. Currently you're ted Terry, novelist of the trenches and doomed young chaps.

Writer: And? I mean, is that not my brand?

Agent: We thought that Ted Terry, the guy with the German officers…

Writer: Eh?

Agent: Just a change of focus Ted.. give us more Germans.

Writer: Get stuffed. That's not a brand.

Agent: I've upset you Ted… well, if you want to see sales dip, just stick in the mud … (chuckles)

Ted: There are other agents, Peter!

Slams phone down.

Rejection may be totally crushing. In our time, as opposed to the anxious waiting for the heavy package, as was the case with Comstock, the rebuff is likely to be that one sentence or possibly two, and so the wound is not only deep but tormenting. If the rejection is worded simply 'At our meeting, it was decided that this is not for us' or 'Dear Stephen, not this time I'm afraid' then what follows? It is the anguish of not knowing why you have produced a dud. Both fiction and non-fiction have their own species of pain. The novelist has submitted perhaps three chapters and has probably written virtually all the book, whereas the non-fiction writer has sent a proposal and maybe two chapters. That short stab of rejection commits the text to oblivion. Over the years, as a creative writing tutor, I have had hundreds of students lament their drawers full of aborted novels- lots of files containing three chapters and a synopsis, frozen in that limbo of dead would-be novels.

I have wandered around, dazed and confused, after being told that my 8,000 words of narrative, the product of sweatshop labour at the screen, were not wanted, not up to the mark, did not inspire, failed to excite, and similar. Increasingly, I have come to realise that we scribblers are all bonkers, going alone into a room to tell lies to a screen and call it inspiration

8

BEING PROFESSIONAL

It was in the last years of the nineteenth century that authors really had the chance to get some support from a proper professional organisation: The Society of Authors was formed in 1884, with Walter Besant as the leading light. Two years later there was the first International Copyright Convention at Berne. An anonymous writer published these lines in *The World* magazine:

> ' Some literary gents the other day did meet
> *All in a private chamber, which looks on Garrick*
> *Street;*
> *There they did meet together, and solemnly they swore*
> *That as they had been done enough they would be*
> *done no more.*'

Previously, and in fact still for some time after until the law really had an impact, writers had had the most horrendous experience in trying to preserve their rights to their work. Most bizarre of all was probably the story of Gilbert and Sullivan, who had such an immense success with *The Pirates of Penzance* that they were exploited and copies done. All a rival had to do at that time was sit in a theatre and copy down the dialogue etc. The only ruling at the time was that playwrights had to have two copyrights – as Victor Bonham-Carter explains, '.. playwrights felt obliged to organise 'copyright performances' or public readings of their plays before publication, and book authors would do the same to prevent unauthorised stage versions of their work…'

Still, in the last decades of the nineteenth century there were still authors who struggled. Even R L Stevenson did not write an immediate best-seller. What he did do was make the right contacts: R L S wrote an essay on 'Roads' and it was rejected by *The Saturday Review*. But he had friends, and one was Sidney Colvin, who helped to have it accepted by another magazine. R L S was launched on his career. Yet there was still a struggle. In April 2011, a newspaper announced that a lost Stevenson masterpiece had been found. In fact, this was an unfinished novel called *The Hair Trunk*, and in a letter of 1877 he wrote to a friend, describing his state of mind while writing this, and he was clearly aware that it was likely to fail: ' I'm engaged upon –trumpets, drums- a novel!... It is a most absurd story of a lot of young Cambridge fellows who are going to found a new society…'

Now, thanks to a certain Michel Lebris, the novel has been completed, and printed- in French.

Richard Church- *Rejected with Style*

In the vast literature of writer's memoirs, some very lengthy enterprises have been achieved. These are autobiographies which extend over several volumes, and usually go into considerable depth with regard to the writer's usually steady progress towards being published. One such was Richard Church, who wrote such a trilogy and won a major literary award for *Over the Bridge*. In *The Voyage Home*, he recounts his efforts to succeed where many thousands have tried- in the meetings, clubs, offices and party-times of the London literati. In the course of trying to find a publisher for an epic poem, which is a form almost invariably unfashionable, he gave an account of surely the most nervous, lengthy and in the end very stylish rejection on record. This was in 1920, a time when the great modernists were coming through, so it was a time for experiment and for trying to be different.

He approached a small publisher called Roger Ingpen, and then received a note asking him to meet the publisher in his offices. Church gave a reading that day, but he was a bundle of nerves: 'A sense of foreboding prevented me from concentrating my attention on the shelves of riches before which I stood unsteadily…' He was cold and hungry as he walked at dusk to meet Ingpen, and he walked with him to his office, nothing being said about the manuscript. Then, the publisher diverted all attention away from the discussion of the poem by producing the actual notebook that had been in Shelley's possession when he drowned at sea in 1822.

With this startling talking-point, who was to mention Church's epic poem? The lack of a response went on, but then: ' There was a long pause, as after a church service, then Ingpen took up an all too familiar parcel from his desk. 'I'm afraid,' he said, looking from left to right and right to left, 'That this is beyond our resources. You see, the length...' It was a moment similar to the dramatic criticism given by the Emperor Joseph to one of Mozart's symphonies: 'too many notes.' This angle on the criticism of art was always taken up in my family whenever a play extending more than a reasonable time was being watch. My mother would say, 'Well, it's good, but it's on too long.'

Joseph Conrad Almost Kills his own Career

In that age of bookmen, the booming 1890s and the next twenty years, when Church was active, there were plenty of publishers looking for fiction, and the professional reader emerged also. The publishers needed readers to write critiques of work, and of course, to find new authors of merit.

Edward Garnett, the doyen of readers in that age, was given the task of advising Joseph Conrad, the seaman-novelist who had chosen to write in his third language- English- having been born Josef Korzeniowski in Poland, and having French as his second language. In several years of sailing around the world as a professional mariner with a master's certificate, he elected to try his hand at fiction. The result was a four-year project resulting in his first novel, *Almayer's Folly*. While it was in progress, and he was serving as first mate on the Torrens, a celebrated ship which made many trips to Australia and back, he did what most tyro writers long to do but seldom have the courage to see through: he showed a chapter to a stranger, a man called Jacques, as he recounts in his book, *A Personal Record*:

> 'Well, what do you say, I asked at last. 'Is it worth finishing?'

'Distinctly', he answered in his sedate, veiled voice, and then coughed a little.

'Were you interested?' I inquired further, almost in a whisper.

'Very much!'

'Now let me ask you one more thing: is the story quite clear to You, as it stands?'

He raised his dark, gentle eyes to my face and seemed surprised.

'Yes, perfectly.

This was all I was to hear from his lips concerning the merits of *Almayer's Folly*. We never spoke of the book again.'

In fact, Jacques died shortly after returning home.

When it was finally finished, off it went to the publisher Unwin, and Conrad, jobless, had a long wait. He wrote one of the most explanatory letters of enquiry on record, after waiting for months and having no decision. In this he says, 'I venture now upon the liberty of asking you whether there is the slightest likelihood of the MS. (Malay life, about 64,000 words) being read at some future time?'

We can positively sense the frustration behind this polite request. It has that familiar ring of desperation mixed with fear that such a communication tends to have. It was posted on 8 September, 1894 and two days later he received an acceptance. Then followed a strange scene. He was called to meet Garnett and the publisher At the meeting, in a literary club in which other writers were present, Unwin asked when he was to write the next novel? Allegedly, in one of many slightly conflicting versions, Conrad said something that your average struggling scribe would never, ever say. He said, I don't expect to write again. It is likely that I shall be going to sea!'

Still, all turned out well in the end, and Conrad had the itch to write that all compulsive storytellers know. He was soon at work on what was to become *An Outcast of the Islands*.

G.B.S Struggles

One final case study in rejection will show the depths to which failure may reach. This is the story of how one of the greatest of all dramatists in history began as an unwanted novelist. George Bernard Shaw. In 1879, desperately trying to find print, he wrote manically on virtually everything under the sun. In March that year he started work on a novel called *Immaturity*, and he called it his 'first attempt to write a big book' working methodically, producing five hand-written pages a day. He finished it in September, and then worked on revisions. By November it was ready to be taken to the offices of a publisher, and it was rejected within a week.

More ruthless rebuffs were to follow. He fancied himself as a music critic so he approached the editor of the *Pall Mall Gazette* and the rejection included advice- that he would be much better off not doing any journalism at all. He doggedly started on his next novel, working very hard. It was called *The Irrational Knot* and was rejected mainly because the publisher thought it to be immoral.

By 1882 he completed his next failure: *Love Among the Artists,* and it was submitted to publishers, Fisher Unwin. Their reader was Edward Garnett, friend of D H Lawrence and a writer himself. His rejection letter reads almost like an acceptance, hence displaying the complex art of clever refusal: 'The literary art is sound, the people in it are real people, and the fresh unconventionality is pleasing after the ordinary work of the common novelist, but all the same, few people would understand it and few papers would praise it.' He thought that Shaw's work would not 'command much attention.' How wrong can a man be!

His fourth novel, *Cashel Byron's Profession*, was completed by February, 1883. He had also been maintaining his programme of self-education, working in the British Museum, eating sparingly and visiting art galleries. He also loved boxing, and the new novel was set in the world of pugilism. Everyone turned it down. Michael Holroyd, Shaw's biographer, comments that Macmillan's reader decided that is was '... well and brightly written, but the subject is not likely to commend itself to any considerable public.' Not to be deterred, Shaw pressed on, and produced the next novel, *An Unsocial Socialist.* Again the responses were negative.

Michael Holroyd stresses just how much poor Shaw found the energy and stamina to carry on, and he quotes a letter from Shaw written to Macmillan, which might stand as the expression of the failure's plight for all aspiring authors. In the letter he wrote, 'Surely out of thirty millions of copyright persons there must be a few thousand who could keep me in bread and cheese for the sake of my story-telling, if only you would let me get at them.'

As is well known, the end of the story is that Shaw really made it as a writer. Not long after these struggles with fiction, he was writing for the *Pall Mall Gazette* and then his book *The Quintessence of Ibsenism*, made him something of a celebrity.

There was a capacity for hard work and also plenty of talent in Shaw, and his story of rejection and persistence is surely a model for all who aspire to be writers.

Even his fiction found print eventually: he merely took a rather long and painful route to success. One thing in Shaw's experience provides sound advice to writers: be like a dog with a bone when you believe in your script: keep hold of it.

Using Failure to Succeed

Combing the massive annals of the history of literature in search of notable failure, I came across some outstanding examples of writers who approached the whole business with an enviable methodology. They may have flopped in the first phase of activity, but their masterplan worked in the end. If I had to choose a quintessential example of this admirable approach it would be the career of Yorkshire novelist and author of *A Kind of Loving,* Stan Barstow. He died in 2011, after a long career as writer and teacher of writing.

I met Stan in 1985 in Calderdale library, not far from his birthplace of Ossett, Wakefield. He gave a talk on writing to my students who were on my Access course at further education college. When I spoke to him and asked for advice, he said, 'Steve, I just write books… fix on one thing. No time for all this article stuff. Fix on one thing and do it to the best of your ability.'

His autobiography, *In My Own Good Time,* shows that he practised what he preached. He started out in life, after grammar school, as a draughtsman in engineering works; then his interest in writing arrived, and he bought a typewriter. With a fine sense of autodidactic endeavour, he read handbooks, took a course, and started writing fiction. He wrote widely on his first efforts: ' I was learning, and the first thing I learned was that even with a reasonably fluent flow of words such as I command, writing insincerely rarely works… I sold nothing in that first phase. The envelopes came back. But I will not say that I wasted valuable time in trying to write what I thought editors would want…'

He persevered, and learned from others the basic wisdom of finding out what kind of writing you actually want to do. He notes that reading H E Bates was the revelation for him – showing him how to write about the people and communities he really knew. By 1954 he first appeared in print, with a short story and after that, the rest is important literary history. He was writing at a time when the northern working class culture and experience was something marketable, but that never drove him to try to write what was beyond him.

Stan had also learned from George Eliot, as he testifies by using these words from her as an epigraph to his memoir: 'A born provincial man who has a grain of public spirit as well as a few ideas should do what he can to resist the rush of everything that is little better than common towards London.' He knew, after a careful study of his chosen craft, that the secret of success at the writing business was to take it seriously, as a journeyman carpenter learns to work with wood and absorb the elements of the trade, steadily and with a sense of purpose.

9

EVEN THE FAMOUS AND SUCCESSFUL ARE REJECTED

The self-help books for aspiring writers insist on reminding us that the path to success is strewn with failures, and that the truly great writers have always met with setbacks. On closer scrutiny, this appears to be generally true. Sometimes these are failings in purely artistic terms, and some help is required to shape up the material into publishable form, as was the case with T S Eliot's great poem, *The Waste Land,* which Eliot was to call He Do the Policeman in Different Voices until his friend Ezra Pound went to work on the typescript and the wonderfully original and starting dramatic poem emerged, to great acclaim. Editors are notoriously helpful, in some celebrated cases, in staving off failure. Another case of this is Scott Fitzgerald's editor, Malcolm Cowley, who did much to refine and revise Fitzgerald's great works.

Yet outright rejection is still very common. One of the most famous poets of the 1960s and 1970s in England, George Mac-

Beth, once told me, after a reading, that one of his collections had done the rounds of 22 publishers – but it made it into print in the end. Nobel Prize winner, Ulster poet Seamus Heaney, as a young man first writing poems, put the name 'incertus' beneath his work: the Latin word for uncertain, hesitant. This introduces the magical, fundamental concept at the heart of both failure and success: confidence and self-belief.

Dylan Thomas was never short of those attributes, yet – although it is hard to believe- he was rejected. In 1933, the bright young lad from Swansea sent poems to Geoffrey Grigson, who was editing the journal, *New Verse*. It was a new publication, with a small circulation, but in the poetry world, it is publication that counts, and an emerging poet needs to develop a c.v. Grigson sent the poems back to Dylan with simply a rejection slip. Still, Dylan had self-belief in abundance, and he was writing drafts in notebooks all the time, as he read and learned. The setbacks happened, but he never lost the sense that he was talented, and that he had to write.

Through success and failure, that message is always there for people to learn from: the writer writes, and that means in spite of rejection and any other problems. The faith, the firm belief, in ability mixes somehow with a sheer addiction to write, and the result is that success is willed, in many cases.

Stories of rejection mostly help to reinforce this view of the craft. A glorious example of this is the rise to fame of Christopher Isherwood. He is mostly known today as the author of the story on which the musical *Cabaret* was based; this is from one of his Berlin stories. Isherwood is a perfect instance of this tendency for failure to play a part in the learning curve. He had been writing fiction since his schooldays, with his friend (and future novelist) Edward Upward. When he set to work on what was to be his first novel, *All the Conspirators*, he was pleased to see it through. Writing in one of his autobiographical works, *Lions and Shadows*, he recalled, '*All the Conspirators...* it sounded grand. True, there was no Anthony in my story, much less a Brutus... but considerations of this sort weighed very little in 1927. *All the Conspirators* was duly sent off on its round of publishers. By Christmas, two had already refused it, with polite regrets.' Then, after Christmas, a letter came from Jonathan Cape publishers: ''Would I go round to see them at once?'

The book made it into print, and Isherwood wrote that he kept going to pick up a copy from his own author's copies and peeping at it, with his name in print. But even that was open to problems: the critics hated it. The worst judgement was perhaps in *Punch*, which had the comment that 'Altogether, the book leaves behind it a faintly nasty taste...'

Undeterred, Isherwood, luckily being able to cash a war bond for £50, set off for Berlin. The rest is literary history, as he was destined to be one of the rising stars of the thirties and forties, along with W H Auden, Stephen Spender and George Orwell.

Very few modern writers have that knack of being so appreciated as a genius that they never know rejection. Take the example of poet Ted Hughes, up at Pembroke College, Cambridge, for instance. He was reputed to be such a great poet that everyone assumed that he would be published, and that his work would be highly acclaimed. When he finally did submit work to an editor (under a nom de plume) it was accepted. His poems were in the magazines *Delta* and *Granta* and so his career was launched. Like Pessoa, he relished the idea of having alter-ego writers with interesting names, so his first name in print was Daniel Hearing.

After that it seemed like a *fait accompli* on the part of all his literary friends that he would soon have a first collection in print. In fact, it took three years: he left university in 1954 and *The Hawk in the Rain* appeared in 1957. But in that period he was involved in magazine publishing, meeting other writers, and keeping busy, although, as his biographer, Elaine Feinstein notes, he was not really concerned with self-promotion. It all seemed to come naturally- as if his decision to be a writer, made when he was a boy, was going to happen, and indeed that destiny was fulfilled.

Joseph Brodsky, in his book of essays, *Less Than One*, opines that the great poet, Anna Akhmatova was of a similar nature: he wrote that she '…belongs to the category of poets who have neither genealogy nor discernible development. She is the kind of poet that simply "happens"; that arrives in the world with an already established diction and his/her own unique sensibility.'

Back in 1827, the Tennyson brood had a similarly easy entrance into authorship. In 1827, the local publishers, Jacksons of Louth, Lincolnshire, brought out the first book in which Tennyson appeared: *Poems by Two Brothers*. He and his brother Charles (and also Fred, the third, but he faded away). Not only did they break into print at a very early age (Tennyson was just 18), but they were actually paid – for poetry! They received £20, £5 of which was in books from Jackson's shop. Once again, Alfred, the future Lord Tennyson, went swiftly into the ranks of the published authors, and with no problems.

EVEN THE FAMOUS AND SUCCESSFUL ARE REJECTED

How different is the situation for most writers, notably in that century since the emergence of Modernism in the first years of the twentieth century. Yet even that revolution in mass media, in the Edwardian years when the periodicals boomed and editors wanted writers to supply the twenty-minute read for the London commuters, appears now to be very limited compared with the world of sound bites, networking and tweets.

In the contemporary world of writing and publishing, the writer has to be many things: publicist, proof-reader, marketing director and oh, yes, writer. The whole business is about adapting to survive. Successful novelist Sarah Harrison explains that in one failed novel she decided to change the nature of the genre by 'boosting the sex content' instead of the usual scene, 'stopping outside the bedroom door.' It worked for her. In contrast, one novelist told me that she wanted to change her well-established saga novel setting of Glasgow and have a story in which her characters emigrated to the USA. She wrote a goodly section of that before being told, 'No… your readers need to have Glasgow in the story… your books are Glasgow books.'

If an example might be needed of a world-famous author who suffered repeated rebuffs and setbacks in his path to writing success, the outstanding example is Hans Christian Andersen. Young Hans, while a poor college student, was desperate to find success as a dramatist. He was supposed to be attending Latin classes, and also classes in singing and dance, but he fell into poverty. He was so naïve that middle class contacts he went to for help were shocked – he plagiarised successful playwrights for instance, and when challenged, said, 'but they are so lovely.'

Hans did write original work, starting with a short play called *The Robbers of Vissenburg*. Alison Prince describes the response to the professionals who received it: ' They turned it down with an exasperated letter which insisted that work betraying such an abysmal lack of education should not be submitted.'

He then produced a five-act tragedy called *Alfsol* and with his usual pushiness he gained a session at home, for time during a family lunch, with a translator called Wulff. Amazingly, Hans used the occasion to read aloud from *Alfsol*. The man forgave the imposition, and still took to Hans – who was only seventeen. Not long after, a scene from his first play was accepted for a magazine. Had he arrived? No. There was still a long way to go. Many years later, in 1834, he finished what was to be his first published work, a novel called *The Improvisatore*. But he had had to pay for its publication, so that does not really count as a success – or does it? The issue is a very contemporary one. In fact, it was a notable success, so it's harsh to label this a sign of failure. Then in May, 1835, four of his stories, the writing that made him famous, were in print.

The point about Hans Andersen's story here is that although he had plenty of learning difficulties, and a tough start in life (his father's insanity being the main cause of problems) he had self-belief, and in fact he also had a clumsy, thoughtless type of selfishness that sometimes impressed.

Gertrude Stein and Mr Fifield

In April, 1912, Gertrude Stein received a rejection letter. She had lived in Paris for ten years, with her brother, Leo, after starting out as a psychology student. In Paris, she carried on the great French tradition of holding a literary salon – ands this was an extraordinary one, with such artists and writers as Picasso, Matisse and Hemingway to drop in for drinks and conversation. In 1907 her friendship with another American, Alice N Toklas, began, and in Stein's classic work, *The Autobiography of Alice B Toklas*, she produced what was to become her classic work, although she wrote in several genres and categories, including a variety of non-fiction.

The letter from Mr Fifield in London may not have pleased the publisher, but it did provoke him to create a stunningly original and strong piece of writing in his rejection letter:

> 'Dear Madam,
> I am only one, only one, only one. Only one being, one at the same time. Not two. Not three. Only one. Only one life to live, minutes in one hour. Only one pair of eyes. Only one brain. Only one being. Being only one, having only one pair of eyes... I cannot read your manuscript Three of four times..... Hardly one copy would sell here....'

It is a template statement from that period in which modernist writing was still slamming up against traditional concepts of what books would sell, and to the middle class reader. Although there had been a boom in all kinds of fiction publishing throughout the Edwardian and neo-Georgian years, the generation of writers following the monumental innovations of Woolf, Eliot and Joyce, still came up against entrenched attitudes and lots of editors and publishers who were stuck in conventional notions of 'what would sell.'

As for Gertrude Stein, her book on Alice made it into print in 1933 and the two women were celebrities. She had been helped also in her difficult period, when she found it hard to find publishers, by Mabel Dodge, who paid for the publication of a limited edition of a book called Portrait of Mabel Dodge at Villa Curonia.

Katherine Anne Porter's comment on Stein's style and approach perhaps explains her experimentation: ' Wise or silly or nothing at all, everything goes on the page with an air of everything being equal, unimportant in itself, important because it happened to her and she was writing about it.' One has to reflect that an editor today would want to get to work on writing like that, and think about a Gertrude Stein brand.

Once again, it is hard to resist the feeling that in the arts, who you know really does count. Gertrude started that salon and, amazingly, a few top-notch creative types, destined for greatness, popped in for a chat. Still, it is hard to resist the thought that, if we tried a salon today in Britain, we would find that only bores, odd-balls and eccentrics would call in, and they wouldn't have any useful contacts. They would all go home and write sarcastic blogs about the lack of intellectual thrust at your *conversazione*. A look at successful literary salons in history suggests that the hostess needs to be only half-dressed, smoke Balkan Sobranis and order the butler to bring a vodka for everyone.

Rejected after the Launch of a Career!

The immensely popular novelist, creator of the Larkin family, H E Bates, had been taken up by Jonathan Cape in the early

1920s, after submitting his second novel. That auspicious start to his career certainly filled him with confidence, and he was fortunate in having that great reader and editor, Edward Garnett, on his side. Not only did Garnett ask the fledgling writer to send him everything else he had in his files, but he also acted as literary agent and placed most of these short pieces in various periodicals.

Everything must have looked rosy and bright, and Bates set out to produce a massive novel he called The Voyagers, stretching to around 120,000 words. He finished it in July, 1927, and in his autobiography, *The Ripening World*, he wrote: ' The long, grinding stint of *The Voyagers* ended...Utterly exhausted, I snatched at the chance of a short holiday in Germany..' He had a good time, and returned with the usual apprehension about his latest script. Garnett had been to work on it, and the worst happened: he hated it. Garnett was an exceptional critic, proud of the fact that he had risen in the publishing industry as a man of letters without a university education (and the same applied to Bates, so they shared something). His letter giving the verdict on Bates' new novel was crushing. Bates wrote:' He wrote not merely that my novel was terrible, but that it simply could not be published. It was written in a "facile, flowing, half-faked style," it was cursed with 'generalities, vague cynicism, washy repetitions.' As Bates summed up: 'In fact, Edward that morning, hit me with everything he'd got.'

Still, there is a lesson to be learned from Bates' full account of this massive failure. Even that damning critique contained one piece of light in the aesthetic bleakness: 'Don't despair. You have a facile demon in you, who gets hold of the reins, as well as the real artist in you, who retreats into the background.' What a wonderfully succinct and wise statement that is: the kind of advice every writer wants to have. Bates was smart enough to see that Garnett had read deeply enough to understand the weakness inherent in Bates' storytelling and the structure he used for its plotting.

This crisis led Bates to a period of soul-searching, looking to understand himself more. The feedback on his work, after so much effort and for so long, was a body-blow, but he had the sense to cling on to the one positive statement. It look a very long time to come through this identity crisis and out into the light again. When he returned to the world of writing, suitably enthused to work his way back, he did it with zeal. He wrote, ' And work like hell I did. Again, often, like Chekhov, I wrote a story between breakfast and lunch, an article between lunch and tea… I wrote until my hands trembled…' Eventually, he completed the next novel, *The Fallow Land*, and he did what most writers do early in their careers- he went deeply into the place of his early life. In this case, it was the Nene Valley. Garnett liked it. Bates was back on course, as he was meant to be.

The twentieth century has lots of cases like this in its literary history, particularly in the 30s and 40s. as this was a time when creative writing boomed and new voices were encouraged. It was a time when publishers and editors were looking for writers from the working classes; the age of documentary writing flourished, and important anthologies such as *New Writing*, edited by John Lehmann, launched many careers, later becoming *Penguin New Writing,* issued in mass paperback format. Becoming a writer – at least as a part-time occupation – seemed a little more of a viable option for working people with a skill in storytelling, and publishers were open to international writing and to innovative narrative.

There was also the genre of autobiography: resulting in more material on the subject of the writer's life. Such topics as writers' block, the imagination, literary influence, and new versions of Modernism, all became prominent. H E Bates was entirely typical of this generation, weaving the story of his writing experience into the wider issues of his time.

10

BAD REVIEWS

Reviewing of new books began in the Regency period, as the new and powerful literary periodicals appeared. Critics appeared – men whom Dr Johnson described as types who became 'important and formidable at very small expense.' The thousands of new writers who thronged into print from the late eighteenth century through to early Victorian times therefore had to face the important verdicts of the reviewers. It may seem odd to talk of such a variety of failure, because the writer's work is in print, but there are versions of success and failure which appear in a number of guises. In 1800 a bad review could be the kiss of death on a writer's reputation – so different from today when we can write our own glowing reviews of course.

The Romantics- and Wordsworth's Bad Reviews

They all either knew each other or they knew of each other; they wrote letters incessantly; they held dinner parties to celebrate a new publication by one of their circle, or they assembled simply to talk- endlessly, entertainingly, and to show off. They cared nothing for any reputation they might have as a coterie: in fact they relished the chance to be talked about and part of their role was scandal and gossip. They were the literary elite of the Regency years, a mix of poetasters, raconteurs, hack reviewers and bookmen. Women were admitted and highly valued and respected as long as they could hold their own in conversation and controversy. They welcomed the chance to lionize a newcomer, as they did with the semi-literate Northamptonshire poet, John Clare. In short, they were the Romantic generation, and among the penny-a-line-men and tattlers there were creative minds of rare genius: writers who are now of classic status. Among these are Byron, Wordsworth, Coleridge and Shelley.

They wrote manically, by sunlight and by candle-light; they lusted for the wilderness and for the city; the mad flux of life in Regency Britain offered them 'subjects' endlessly, as a society looking over the Channel in paranoia expected the death of kings and the triumph of the terror some called Boney to urge their children to sleep. Reputations were forged in jealousy, heart-thumping drive to puff the latest poem, wranglings with the booksellers of St Pauls, and desperate applications to grasp hold of the sinecures that gave the scribbler some freedom to write and afford more wine. More than all these, they wrote with one eye on competition: friendship was often a moveable feast, as poetasters rubbed shoulders with painters at a dinner or a drunken evening in a tavern. The belief in the genius of the solitary artist filtered into their consciousness, with the acute awareness that failure could lead to suicide in an attic, like the end of young Chatterton, madness in Bedlam or oblivion in a debtors' prison. Chancers they were, and they knew it.

Print my sonnets, produce my play, feed my melancholy, lionize that rustic with his rough peasant vernacular, wait at the levee for Milord and write in praise of his dog or his mistress; choose an allegiance, take sides, bite and scratch for a good review from the latest critic in the freshest periodical. Work, create, triumph... or go under. Like my conversation, soothe my ego, laugh at my stories, be my creature, smile and fawn, help me to rise...

Every year brought a richness of new, hot topics, such as who had sunk through debt or who had been accused of sedition. Their world was at war and across the Channel there had been a revolution, and so Westminster looked with fear and paranoia at writers, painters and poets. But there was one year which was to stand out as special: 1814. In that year, Bonaparte finally admitted defeat and slunk off to the island of Elba, and none of them knew how short that respite would be before he returned to threaten the world yet again.

They all either knew each other or they knew of each other; they wrote letters incessantly; they held dinner parties to celebrate a new publication by one of their circle, or they assembled simply to talk- endlessly, entertainingly, and to show off. They cared nothing for any reputation they might have as a coterie: in fact they relished the chance to be talked about and part of their role was scandal and gossip. They were the literary elite of the Regency years, a mix of poetasters, raconteurs, hack reviewers and bookmen. Women were admitted and highly valued and respected as long as they could hold their own in conversation and controversy. They welcomed the chance to lionize a newcomer, as they did with the semi-literate Northamptonshire poet, John Clare. In short, they were the Romantic generation, and among the penny-a-line-men and tattlers there were creative minds of rare genius: writers who are now of classic status. Among these are Byron, Wordsworth, Coleridge and Shelley.

As this was going on, Charles Lamb was busy writing for the reviews, and he had a commission from *The Quarterly Review*, and it was a task he was to find onerous and difficult: the editor ignored Wordsworth's request that Southey write the review, and the job was given to Charles. The book under review was *The Excursion*. This was going to be a delicate task. A writer was used to producing a review of a friend's book – that was the established custom. But there were degrees of affability, charm and sheer toadying. Charles was not the kind to crawl and simper, to ingratiate by oiling the wheels of favouritism. The little man was naturally witty; in company he could be relied upon to have a story that would appeal to all. He was just as handy with an in-joke as he was with a pun. In print he had won his celebrity among his peers by extending that humour and cosy down-playing of any exclusive attitudes; his prose was a kind that any educated reader would appreciate – not peppered with Latin nor with obscure references. His allusions were those shared by his peers. But now here he was faced with the challenge of being what he always was – honest and forthright and with a brief to entertain – but having to write about a work which prompted only lukewarm responses. What was he to do?

He did what the most intelligent critics tend to do – he described and summarised, playing safe with rather reserved compliments, then elaborates: ' To a mind constituted like that of Mr Wordsworth, the stream, the torrent and the stirring leaf – seem not merely to suggest associations of deity, but to be a kind of speaking communication with it.' William would have liked that, but then Charles sets about a comment on a structural, editorial matter: ' ... we could have wished therefore that the tale of Margaret had been postponed, till the reader had been strengthened by some previous acquaintance with the author's theory.' A page later, Charles has to comment with commercial, voguish sentiments in mind, and a criticism is implied: ' The times are past when a poet could securely follow the direction of his own mind into whatever tracts it might lead..... He must not think or feel too deeply.'

That last sentence would have cut William to the quick. After all , *The Excursion* was a part of his great project, *The Recluse*, and the whole point of the enterprise was very deep thinking. Finally, Charles puts his finger on the aspect of Wordsworth's work which was to bring him much more severe criticism: ' One objection it is impossible not to foresee. It will be asked, why put such eloquent discourse in the mouth of a pedlar? ' Charles does not leave it there, though: he provides an answer which would have pleased his friend in The Lakes: 'Is it too much to suppose that the author, at some early period of his life, may himself have known such a person...?'

Even endorsement and media presence attained by powerful and influential people may not guarantee real success. A perfect example is that of the poet Ronald Bottrall, who was a notable success in terms of his writing achievements and diplomatic career. He was awarded an OBE. But strangely Bottrall arguably 'failed' simply in the sense that the great critic F R Leavis first championed his work, and then dropped him. Bottrall was a fine poet and did not deserve this, but such is the unpredictable nature of literary success that at first Leavis included Bottrall in his influential book of 1932, *New Bearings in English Poetry,* and then abandoned him as any kind of bright hope for the future a decade or so later.

This is often found in cases of writers who were very well reviewed in their time but who sank into oblivion (or at least neglect) later. In Macaulay's time, when he was a very powerful reviewer and essayist in the mid-Victorian years, he called this 'puffing' and wrote about the case of a poet called Robert Montgomery. Such was the furore at the time about the media hype about his work, that in 1830, one Edward Clarkson felt moved to write an entire book on the topic – Robert Montgomery and his Reviewers, published in 1830. Clarkson writes there that ' The great popularity of Mr Montgomery's next work, The Omnipresence of the Deity, which passed through ten editions with unequalled rapidity, demonstrated that the public, in no small measure, sympathised with that appreciation…They have convinced me that the poet is possessed of that true, original creative power which constitutes that of a genius of the first order…'

We can see from this just how powerful reviews were by that time. Not long before that book, when John Keats was alive and writing, there was one of the most celebrated regimes by reviewers against contemporary writers: that of *Blackwood*'s writers in particular against what they called 'The Cockney School' of poets. They referred to Keats, Leigh Hunt and others, and did so largely in terms of a dislike of their class background. Such was the acrimony involved that one reviewer, John Scott, was killed in a duel with an agent of John Lockhart, in 1821.

The first attack on the 'Cockney' poets appeared in Blackwood's Edinburgh Magazine in 1817. and John Lockhart was in the vanguard of the attackers. As Daisy Hay comments in her biography of the poets involved, ' When *Endymion* was published in the spring of 1818, Blackwood's pulled it apart before it had any chance of reaching a sympathetic readership..' This certainly had a profound effect on Keats.

The Powerful Bookmen

In his exhaustive study of powerful literary men (they tended to be male) throughout the nineteenth and twentieth centuries, John Gross gives plenty of examples of how far reviews could make a book fail and ruin a reputation. But ironically, one of the most celebrated reviewers of the time, Francis Jeffrey, was not exactly a raging success as a creative writer himself. Gross writes: 'In his early twenties his hopes were set on a poet's career, although only his family were allowed to inspect his first shy efforts; and 1,800 line fragment of blank verse on 'Dreaming', a handful of landscape-sketches and lyrics.' Clearly he was a failed writer and so he concentrated on destroying the reputations of other writers.

However, it is hard to deny that reviewing then (and now) has another aspect, and this is important. As John Gross puts it: 'There were powerful voiced raised throughout the Victorian period, inveighing against the pursuit of second-rate novelty, exhorting readers not to waste their time on anything less than the best, the *very* best…' The problem with this is that some reviewers tend to express opinion rather than informed judgement. The case of a review of Vladimir Nabokov's *Lolita* in 1958 shows this: 'Dull, dull, dull in a pretentious, florid and archly fatuous fashion' wrote the reviewer for *The New York Times*.

As the years have rolled on since those first influential periodicals of the eighteenth century, the issue as far as writers are concerned is concerned with the qualifications of reviewers. In other words, there are amateurs involved, just as there are in the judging panel for the Man Booker Prize. The question arises: should book reviewers be successful writers in the category or genre of the book they write about? The old argument in defence of the critic would be that of Samuel Johnson, who said that though he may not be able to make a good table, he knew a good table when he saw one. This is debateable of course.

Today, as reviews in papers and journals have diminished in number, they have less effect on a writer's career. Far more important is the decision of the online community. The modern writer blogs, tweets and keeps updated on Facebook, in addition to pressing for media presence at every opportunity. He or she can write their own reviews and in fact, fabricate a complete profile for the book in question.

In addition to this, we are all potentially publishers now. A self-published e-book is not the only work of tee author; all related copy is also supplied, from blurb to material that would normally be written for a publisher on a proposal or synopsis pro forma. Still, reviewing does have an influence, particularly in a double page feature in a weekend magazine or in a tabloid daily.

My Part in Failure by Review

In my writing career, I have reviewed probably around 200 books. I have written for *Times Literary Supplement, Times Higher Education, Books and Bookmen, Agenda* and many more. My policy always was that I would not write a review which would attack and harshly criticise a book. If I disliked a book, my review would look for the good points, and adverse comment would always be explained.

If I reverse this, consulting my file of reviews I have kept of my own work, I find that there are some which affected me and made me reflect on my writing in a useful way. But I have had adjectives applied which stick and still give a little shiver of displeasure: *pretentious, flat* and a more explanatory phrase, '*some parts will be less absorbing.*' On the other hand, the best review (in the form of a letter) I ever had, and it did its part in staving off a feeling of failure, was from a schoolgirl in class 4G:

Dear Steve,

Thank you very much for your time with us. We all enjoyed it very much. We hope that you will be able to come and see us again. We especially liked the penguins. Good luck with your book....'

I have no recollection of the penguins. Did I escort a few polar birds, with Chaplinesque gait, (the birds, not myself) into and infants' school? Or did I merely take in some chocolate snacks?

Women Reviewed Less than men?

In 2011, Jim Behrle responded to a piece by Jodi Picoult in *The New York Times Book Review* relating to a survey and statistics on the under-representation of women in periodicals. Picoult's main point was that chick-lit and women's fiction had very little column space in the journal in question. Behrle commented that he had his doubts, '... about this type of counting project in the past, and I've wondered before if men are just overwhelmingly submitting more work to literary magazines and are therefore being accepted more.'

The response filled around a dozen pages on the Hairpin web site (at http://thehairpin.com) and seems clear that there is a strong and widespread opinion that there is a perceived hierarchy of perceived importance regarding categories of writing, and maybe the old contrast between literary and genre writing is a factor too. Some of the ratios quoted from the survey by VIDA (the Women in Literary Arts site) are uncomfortable reading in a literary world supposedly now defined as equable and open to change: *The New Republic's* ratio was 55 reviews of books by men as opposed to nine by women. Similarly, *The New Yorker's* was 33-9 and *The New York Review of Books* was 306-9. These figures are from 2010.

Yet researchers have claimed that the bias or lack of representation has been there for a very long time and still persists. Behre also suggests that 'perhaps men are less afraid of being rejected, more willing to put themselves out there...' Maybe there are two factors here, then: one is that there is an individuated element, in which some kind of gender-related attitude comes in; the other is simply about power structures in the publishing world.

In contrast to the VIDA findings, I did a sample check on issues of *The New Statesman* in 2013 and found that their average issue contained ten reviews, of which seven were written by men, but on the other hand, each issue featured a quite substantial space given to features on women's writing. One main feature, for instance, was a full page on the American novel, with Renata Adler given most prominence as 'the godmother of a new generation of postmodernists.'

At the same time, *The Times Literary Supplement* reported on VIDA's latest report, noting again that the material 'highlighted an imbalance between the number of female and male reviewers appearing in book pages in England and America. *The Guardian* also joined in, and found that *The London Review of Books* was the main culprit, and the *TLS* noted that 'One *LRB* reader, the novelist Kathryn Heyman, wrote to the magazine to explain her failure to renew her subscription, writing that 'My husband and I play the hilarious poker game "Guess the Ladies" .... We can no longer tolerate the tedium with which we are able to predict the outcomes.'

A wider aspect of this is what Cyril Connolly once described by means of an image, suggesting that if there is a pram in the hall, there is not poet in the house. If we extend this to what has been more recently discussed as a question of 'motherhood and writing' then we have a cause of failure in the world of writing that relates to a very modern dilemma. This is also universal, as may be noted in an interview when a question was asked of Turkish writer Elif Shafak about her book, *Black Milk*: The book refuses to tie up the question of motherhood and writing...' Her reply was:

> 'Absolutely. In Turkey, though not only in Turkey, the pressure on women is tremendous: 'When are you going to have kids? When are you going to get married? Politicians talk about it on TV. It's very hard for women to retain their autonomy. I wanted to show respect for an array of choices and ways of living...'

Naturally, history shows us how the dominance of men in publishing and journalism, established throughout the nineteenth century, had a far-reaching impact and took a long time to be eroded. John Gross's book, referred to above, which recounts 'literary life since 1800' and was published in 1969, has a huge index of writers discussed, and of these several hundred, only eight names are female.

This survey of reviewing makes George Eliot's achievement all the more impressive. She was Mary Ann Evans, writing with a male *nom de plume*, as the Brontes originally did.

She was scholarly, and initially worked in the lower levels of writing, working in translation, but managed to be employed as assistant editor on the *Westminster Review* in 1851, and then became a fiction writer, having her first stories published in *Blackwood's Magazine* by 1857. But such figures stand out as being remarkably exceptional. There is no doubt, after the effects of the vast literature of feminism applied to literature has shown, that failure and rejection has been experienced more widely and sharply by women. As C Shae wrote in an article called 'High Rates of Suicide in Female Writers' when summing up the reasons why so many women writers have taken their own lives: ' Their suicides are the end result, the culmination of an intense personal battle…. The oppressive social conditions which demand her to be a home-maker as well as her own motherly instinct, are all crippling roadblocks to the creation of a magnum opus.' The article also reminds us that, in the case of Anne Sexton's suicide, 'It was later revealed that her immediate family had all but rejected her because of her revealing poems.'

The status and power of reviewing will always be a hot topic. After all, books have landed on editors' desk in great numbers for centuries now, since the first mass periodicals that reviewed new publications – going back to the gentleman's magazine in the late eighteenth century and then the arrival of *Blackwoods* and the *Edinburgh Review*. Looking to the positive, a glance at the career of Cynthia Ozick shows that it is possible for a women writer to be very prominent and successful in the world of the higher journalism. When her most successful work of fiction, *The Shawl*, was published in 1989 she was interviewed, and the readers learned that 'Ever since she started receiving notice about two decades ago-after labouring unrewarded and unpublished for about as long – her characters have appeared to be opposites of herself.'

Cynthia Ozick is now very much the equal of many of the renowned American intellectuals who are able to write on virtually anything, and in the more serious publications, as well as being a powerful force in book reviewing. She is one of the few authors whose essays and reviews are published in book form, such is her following among British and American readers. Yet she has said that 'I have to talk myself into bravery with every sentence-sometimes every syllable' as quoted in *The Courage to Write* by Ralph Keyes.

This wide-ranging survey has avoided the simple question: does a bad review mean literary failure? The example of Wordsworth's *The Excursion* I discussed earlier in the chapter shows that, if an author is sensitive enough, then the answer might be yes. A comforting thought, though, is that most famous writers have carried on after unpleasant and discouraging reviews. But a final footnote to the history of reviews and reviewing has to be given. A look at the letters pages of *The Times Literary Supplement* demonstrates the fact that writers do read their reviews

– and that they tend to answer back, and take issue with verdicts given against them.

A typical response letter might be something like this:

Dear Editor,
Has your reviewer read my book? Perusing her review of my new history of Tree-felling in Siberia, I have to suggest that she merely skimmed the text, as her Review is riddled with inaccuracies and distortions….

Of course, in the twenty-first century there are ways and means to ensure that a book does not fail because of a bad review. As Alison Flood wrote in an article on the ethics of book reviews: a friend of hers was offered a 'nice' review of her new novel as long as she paid the book review blog $95.

www.ingramcontent.com/pod-product-compliance
Lightning Source LLC
Chambersburg PA
CBHW061604110426
42742CB00039B/2774